Our Debt to Greece and Rome

EDITORS

GEORGE DEPUE HADZSITS, PH.D.

University of Pennsylvania

DAVID MOORE ROBINSON, PH.D., LL.D.

The Johns Hopkins University

O città graziosa à ciascuna nazione per lo tuo cittadino!

BOCCACCIO

OVID
AND HIS INFLUENCE

BY

EDWARD KENNARD RAND

PROFESSOR OF LATIN

Harvard University

LONGMANS, GREEN AND CO.
55 FIFTH AVENUE
NEW YORK
1928

RAND
OVID

THE PLIMPTON PRESS · NORWOOD · MASSACHUSETTS
PRINTED IN THE UNITED STATES OF AMERICA

To

MY WIFE

PREFACE

OUR debt to Ovid! What, save the warning of an awful example, does our age owe to a professed *roué*, the author of a monument so dangerously typical of his degenerate society that the ruler of Rome banished him to a frozen land and excluded his book from the libraries? It would seem as if Ovid's influence ended and ought to have ended then and there. Somehow it has survived. In certain momentous periods of human history, Ovid's name has shone brightly among the immortals. Part of his fame, of course, is due to other works besides the *Art of Love*. It may be, further, that Augustus and the Puritans of his time, and the Puritans of other times, did not quite understand the qualities of that poem or the character of its author. Ovid is nothing if not subtle, nor had he any desire to present his apologies to those who could not see what he was about. Moralists have put him on their black list again and again. His art, too, has seemed to many steeped in rhetoric and thoroughly insincere. According to Mr. Palgrave, no mean judge of letters, he is "amongst world-famous poets, perhaps the least true to the soul of poetry." Today, in our own country certainly, he is hardly more than a school-book. He has surmounted the Alps of the centuries *ut declamatio fiat*. His own imagination could have contrived no more horrible metamorphosis than this. But why should one try to revive him? What is our debt to him?

CONTENTS

[ix]

CONTENTS

ILLUSTRATIONS

[xi]

OVID AND HIS INFLUENCE

OVID AND HIS
INFLUENCE

I. OVID IN THE WORLD OF
POETRY

Nimium amator ingenii sui. QUINTILIAN
Ingenio perii Naso poeta meo. OVID

OVID'S birth in the year 43 B.C. coincides with the beginning of a new age in Roman literature. Virgil, whatever he may have written in his youth, was at work on his *Eclogues*, which both marked an epoch in pastoral poetry and presented a programme of universal peace through Roman imperialism that was destined to become the watch-word of the age and the ideal of its ruler. Ovid was still in his teens when the *Georgics* appeared, in which the idealization of Italy and a " mirror of the prince," — not yet known as Augustus — were even more splendidly displayed. But when the greatest work of the poet, the goal of his aspiration and the complete symbol of the Augustan Age had, after his death in 19 B.C., been given to the world,

[3]

Ovid was already busied with poetry of a very different sort. Horace had described the Roman world, and the world of humanity, in a new and genial satire. He had enticed Aeolian song into Italian measures in a new and Roman lyric, and succeeded Virgil as the laureate of Rome. Ovid, a youth of the rising generation, did not aspire to this part. He has been called, in an admirable work in the present series,[1] " the least Roman of all the Latin poets." Perhaps we should allow Ovid to enlarge our ideas of what " Roman " means; for the old Romans were also Italians. It is true, at any rate, that Ovid's poetry is primarily the expression of his own temperament rather than of some national desire into which his temperament has been caught up. He writes rather as a citizen of the cosmos than as a subject of imperial Rome.

Ovid's native place, Sulmo, lay in a region, now called the Abruzzi, that even today stirs longings for the romantic and the wild. The poet did not forget his birthplace; he revisited it and in his latest poetry cherishes its memory with affection. But though the scenes of his boyhood may have aroused his imagination, they failed to give it a romantic caste. Ovid was fascinated with the novelty of adventure, but no adventure controlled him. He loved nature and could paint her finest shadings, but he never confused himself with meadow, stream or grove. If he ever sought moral lessons, it was not in an impulse from the vernal woods. His soul possessed emotions, but he was the captain of his soul. He was Horace's first pupil, and his aptest, in the golden principle of *nil admirari*. And the Stoic sage, master of the perturbations of the mind, could have profitably sat at Ovid's feet.

Ovid's father, like Petrarch's, destined his son to a career of practical success. The young man obediently started out on this career and disobediently abandoned it. He held various minor judicial posts, but he spent less time at court than with the young poets about town. Ovid, though in command of his moods, was not a poet of solitude; he liked companionship and doubtless made a good *flaneur*. One of his friends, Bassus, was writing stinging iambics. Macer and Ponticus were following the popular trend to epic, with an eye, if they were wise, to the epic achievements of Augustus. The fourth of his intimates was Propertius, already noted for his love-elegies, which set forth, in intensely serious verse, the bitter-sweet of his

passion for Cynthia. Love was a theme well
fitted to Ovid's tastes; he tried his hand at
that. He probably was still under twenty when
the streets of Rome were ringing with his songs
of Corinna, a person mysterious, as we shall
see. But Ovid, no less than Virgil or Milton,
had visions of some greater work ahead. His
earliest plan was for something epic, an heroic
treatment of the battle of the Gods and the
Giants. Horace had shown how this theme
could symbolize the victory of Augustus's
angels over the devils of Antony. It were
strange if this was the only poem for which
Ovid later repented, but as to what these youthful efforts may have been, we have not the
slightest scrap of positive evidence. The epic
was not a success, and the poet returned to
Corinna.

Ovid's first experiments in poetry were preceded, or accompanied, by a thorough training
in the rhetoricians' schools. His masters were
the Spaniard Porcius Latro and Arellius Fus-
cus, an adept in Asiatic exuberance. From
them Ovid learned all the rules of the game.
He sometimes displays his craft too freely, to
the detriment of true feeling and good taste.
But he always has the upper hand. Ovid is

mastered no more by rhetoric than by romantic *Sehnsucht*. If he played with the devices unseasonably and pursued them to extravagance, he knew, like Euripides, what he was about. The elder Seneca [2] tells a delightful story about three kindly critics who pointed out the poet's short-comings and requested the privilege of excising a certain three verses, in different poems, really too bad to stand. Ovid instantly complied, with the stipulation that he should retain a certain three verses, of which he was particularly fond. When both the selections were compared, they were found to be the same. *Non ignoravit vitia sua,* says Seneca, *sed amavit.*

Ovid's best teacher was his own genius. Poetry came to him with an almost fatal ease. Given a theme in prose, he would find that the thing turned out verse. The experience is rare, though repeated by Pope and Lamartine. One of the ancient lives of Ovid declares that once when his father caught him writing a poem and proceeded to apply the rod, the lad cried out (in his native medium):

Parce mihi numquam versificabor pater!

> *Oh father dear, make it no worse;*
> *I vow I'll nevermore write verse!*

[7]

This promise was ill kept. Throughout his life, Ovid's thought flowed into verse, in love-elegy, in tragedy, in tragical monologues of deserted heroines, in an art of cosmetics, in an art of love, in a remedy for the disease, in an epic on miraculous transformations, in a calendar of the Pagan Year. Even after his exile in 8 A.D. to the frozen shore of the Euxine Pontus, his vein of poetry did not freeze. He poured forth laments and petitions for forgiveness, as well as less gloomy strains.

Ovid was thrice married, finding at last a true mate, to whom he writes from exile in terms of deep affection. By one of his earlier wives he had a daughter who imitated the paternal example by marrying twice. One of the letters from exile is addressed to Perilla, probably his step-daughter, the daughter of his third wife. The letter reveals a delightful intimacy between Ovid and the girl; he had encouraged her in the old days to write verse, and had acted as her kindly critic.

The life of our poet, we see, is bisected, like the life of Cassiodorus and of Boccaccio. It is natural to divide Ovid's poetry and his temperament into two halves, one gay and active, one sombre and depressed. But though exile was a

grim reality of horror to Ovid, his genius was
steady and normal in its development, and his
strength was only gradually unnerved by the
catastrophe of his latter days. His successes
and his downfall follow, as he saw, from the
same cause, his wit.

1. THE POET OF LOVE

i. CORINNA

Him, who loves always one, why should they call
More constant, than the man loves always all?
COWLEY

Et falso movi pectus amore meum. OVID

THE Roman love-elegy, whatever had preceded it in the later Greek literature, had a rich
and varied history before Ovid. He mentions
his precursors, Gallus, Tibullus, Propertius, in
a kind of apostolic succession, and registers
himself as fourth in the line.[3] Catullus does
not appear, since technically he should not.
Horace quite as justly does not cite him as his
master in lyric poetry. But though Catullus
eludes literary categories with a Protean agil-
ity, we as moderns must reckon with him in
lyric of a kind that Horace could not write,
and in the poetry of a love that none of his
successors could feel. Jean de Meun, in the

heart of the Middle Ages, as he starts to complete the *Romance of the Rose,* does not leave
Catullus out of his galaxy of the poets of love;
he proudly, and truly, adds his own name and
that of Guillaume de Lorris, the author of the
first part of the great Mediaeval mirror of love
and courtesy. The truth is no less apparent to
Ovid, who pays Catullus his tribute in the
proper place.[4] And despite the technical ac-
curacy of Ovid's account of the elegists, it is
also true that Catullus should be acclaimed as
the inventor of the Roman love-elegy. The
history of a passion, the rehearsal of adventures and joys and woes, is clearly the theme
of Catullus, whatever his form of verse be
called. Though his name may not head the
royal four, who will deny, if we turn from the
singers of love to their ladies, that the line of
Lycoris, Delia, Cynthia and Corinna descends
straight from Queen Lesbia? Who would imagine, if we consider Ovid's words, that he and
Catullus celebrated their sweethearts in a different kind of song? The lines on Corinna and
those on Lesbia seem of a piece.[5] If we would
know the real history of Roman elegy and
understand both Ovid and Catullus, *cherchez
la femme!*

But *cherchez Corinne!* She is hard to find. The name is fictitious, as Ovid informs us. What of her nature? What of the poet's passion? He tells us how it came. He finds his couch hard and the bed-clothes restive. A night of insomnia leaves him with aching bones at dawn, — he concludes that he is in love, and reasons that the best way to stand it is to make no protest. Unconditional surrender to Cupid! Let us celebrate a *trionfo d' amore,* the little god riding in his car, Compliments, Confusion and Craze parading in the van, Conscience and Common Sense trailing behind with shackled wrists, — and there is the poet, the latest catch, trudging along with his fellow-captives.

Think back from this gay imagery to the crystal-clear passion of Catullus:[6]

> I *hate and love. The cause I cannot tell,*
> But *know the feeling and its torture well.*

We need no formal proof that that poet is in love. Tibullus and Propertius took love seriously, a bit too seriously. Ovid's chief inspiration for something new in elegy came from Horace, who finds Tibullus a trifle lacrimose and genially ridicules the lover and his woes. Horace also understands the admirably pro-

[11]

tective art of satirizing the third person in
terms of the first; he did not really blurt out
the story of his love when the wine went to his
head or really lay his plump body on the cruel
sill for an unheeded serenade in the rain. In
such pictures as these, he is having a little fun
with the romantic lover as he appears in elegy;
and Ovid is having more. With an undeniable
interest, and perhaps some experience, in intrigue, with an incorrigible indecency and yet
without a touch of the prurience of Sterne,
he invents a mistress and a world of escapades,
partly to give his fancy rein and partly to in-
dulge in sprightly travesties. *Falsus amor*,
" imaginary amours," is his name for this invention.[7] His amusement must have been vast
when one Roman dame let it be whispered that
she was the genuine Corinna.

Let us follow some of the episodes in our
lover's uncertain career. After his capture, the
new victim takes vows of perpetual fidelity to
his only sweetheart, and promises her through
his songs the immortality of the famous
heroines of myth. In the next poem, he blithely
instructs her how to deceive her husband at a
banquet that they all attend. Then Corinna
comes to him for a mid-day revel. May the

gods send many mid-days of this kind! And
now the lover is singing a sweetly elaborate
serenade, — what is technically known as a
" closed-door serenade " — but it has no effect
on the lady or on the boorish concierge. Our
hero, thus flouted, is desperate. Small wonder
that in a fit of indignation he grabbed his sweetheart and scratched her face; a poem records
his utter repentance and humiliation. Then follows a dreadful scene, witnessed by the poet
behind the arras. The hag Dipsas, procuress
and type of all evil, instructs his darling in the
art of love. The creature's *nomen* is her *omen;*
Dipsy is her name and *tipsy* is her nature.

Ne'*er has Aurora gilt the morning skies*
T*hat Dipsy sighted her with sober eyes.*

She explains the social standards of the age:

T*he slattern Sabine under Tatius' rule*
K*ept but one lover in her simple school.*
W*hile Mars abroad fighteth our foemen down*
G*ood Venus reigns within Aeneas' town.*
O*ur beauties are at play, and she is chaste*
W*hom none has asked. Or if she's not straight-*
     laced,
A *rustic hoyden, she herself will ask.*

[13]

Casta est quam nemo rogavit, — that motto heads one of the stories of Prosper Mérimée and is elaborated wittily by Congreve. It is not the poet's doctrine. Oh, no! Dipsas is the speaker. But from other poems, it is fairly apparent that *rusticitas* is the ultimate word for moral evil, physical evil and spiritual evil. Finally, when the hag exhorts her pupil always to demand pay for her favors, and in particular to set no commercial value on the only coin that the poet can pay, his verses, then his righteous indignation can stand no more. He leaps from his covert and pronounces on the beldame the most awful imprecation that mind can conceive:

> *Homeless and poor, by every god accursed,*
> *Have winters lengthy, and perpetual thirst!*

A dirge now follows, on the loss of his mistress's hair, in consequence of a violent application of cosmetic. But weep no more, Lady, weep no more. Augustus has vanquished the Sygambri, and there should soon come from the north a new supply of wigs in your favorite shade of blonde.

> *Now Germany shall send you caitiff hair;*
> *Thus shall my darling in the triumph share.*

As beaux stand round with admiration big,
Blushing you'll say, " My charm is but a wig.
Some dimpled Gretchen from beyond the Rhine
Merits the fame that once, alas, was mine."

Such is our lover's career. After many successes, after loving two sweethearts at the same time, after loving with undivided affection each girl that he sees, after many buffetings and floutings, he would fain resign. He has had much to bear. It is not pleasant to sing a closed-door serenade to your mistress while the rival is within or to be observed by the latter as he comes away.

Waste no more honeyed words, fell charm of yore.
I'm not so foolish as I was before.

And yet, the battle of Hate versus Love torments him:

I cannot live or with you or without.
I think I know my will and still I doubt.

If only she were either less beautiful or more virtuous, — but either wish is vain. Ah, well, there is no escape.

You're mine, whatever else. Decree my fate!
Will you by will I love, or forced by fate?
But no! Let freedom's breeze my broad sails fill!
I'll nolens volens will Love rule my will!

[15]

This is a complex sort of freedom, worthy a place among the metaphysical conceits of Donne or Cowley. There is an unexpectedly Calvinistic ingredient in Ovid's erotic philosophy; he finds no difficulty in being damned for the glory of his mistress. To die in her embraces, that is the happy end.

Then at the grave some sobbing friend shall say,
" Just as he lived, our Ovid passed away."

ii. THE BEGINNINGS OF A GREATER PLAN

> O mihi tum si vita supersit
> Tu procul annosa pendebis fistula pinu
> Multum oblita mihi. MILTON

> Pulsanda est magnis area maior equis. OVID

Medea

In one of the poems of the *Amores,* Ovid describes the ancient and solemn rites of Juno which he witnessed with his wife at Falerii, a town just over the Etruscan border. The sudden revelation of Ovid as a sober family man taking a steep road to attend a religious festival is a bit disconcerting. Yet the tone of the poem is serious or even devout; Ovid, like a true Roman, has a relish for liturgy.

[16]

'Tis worth the toil to see a splendid rite,
Though rough the hills that take us to the sight.

As the horrors of tragedy are lightened — and intensified — by scenes of comic relief, so there is a kind of " serious relief," the use of which Ovid well understands. Satire, said Thackeray, must walk arm in arm with Sympathy. Humor needs pathos to give it depth, and the audacity of Ovid's wit calls loudly for sobriety. The poet sometimes hears, and sometimes does not heed. The threnody on the death of Tibullus in the *Amores* is spoiled of its seriousness by over-pretty conceits and the amusing cat-fight of Delia and Nemesis at their lover's funeral. One often asks of Ovid, with Dryden, " If this were wit, was this a time to be witty? " Wit, as Ovid observed, was his undoing.

None the less, at the time when our poet was busied with the adventures of his imaginary Corinna and her ridiculous lover, he was planning greater things. The new work should be not epic, for he had burned his fingers in that fire, but tragedy. Ovid was fond of the drama, as allusions in the *Tristia* and adaptations in the *Metamorphoses* amply show. His play, on the familiar subject of Medea, has not

[17]

come down to us, but it won the plaudits of
competent critics like Tacitus and Quintilian.
With the help of Seneca's tragedy on the same
theme, it is perhaps possible to infer that the
conception of Medea in Ovid's play was more
stern and heroic than that which appears in
his later works.

Heroides

O sely womman, ful of innocence,
Ful of pitee, of trouthe, and conscience,
What maked yow to men to trusten so?   CHAUCER

Ignotum hoc aliis ille novavit opus.   OVID

Whatever the merits of his play, Ovid was
not encouraged to send others in its train. Instead, he hit on a happy device, of which a
suggestion had appeared in Propertius, where-
by both his interest in tragedy and his wit,
wholesomely sobered, could find scope. He invented a series of letters, sent by lonely or
desperate heroines to the men who had caused
their distress. The poems are tragic monologues in form, set over into epistles. Attic
tragedy has furnished Ovid with the largest
number of his subjects, yet some come from
epic, some can be traced no farther back than
the Hellenistic period in Greek literature, and

once, in the letter of Dido, the poet reckons
with an illustrious Roman model.

In spirit, only two of these pieces are within
range of tragic feeling. The despair of Phyllis,
nine times descending to the shore and nine
times hoping vainly for the sight of her return-
ing lover's sails, stirs deeper emotions than
mere sympathy. So do the horror and the
bravery of Canace, victim of her brother's incestuous love, and of her own. The former
story, so far as we know, is no earlier than the
Hellenistic age, when tragedy had virtually
ceased to be. Canace was one of the themes of
Euripides, Ovid's master in many ways; one
can feel Greek iambics under the elegiac dis-
tichs at the close of the poem.

Elsewhere in the *Heroides,* one waits in vain
for the thrill of tragic pity and fear, even in
the letters of Medea, Deianira and Phaedra,
heroines that figure in well-known masterpieces
of the Attic stage. Ovid subjects the characters
of tragedy to his art of metamorphosis, as his
predecessors in the Hellenistic age had done.
Heroic figures were made over for romance
then as in the Middle Ages. He was a startling
inventor who in Ovid's phrase,

Made fierce Achilles sentimental.

[19]

Ovid liked the novelty, and tried his hand at it. But there is not the faintest breath of romantic quaintness in his *lettres des dames du temps jadis*. Ovid's is not a chronicle of wasted time, or

> B*eauty making beautiful old rhyme*
> I*n praise of ladies dead, and lovely knights.*

He invites the romantic into the light of common day; his pathos is human and contemporary. It is varied enough; it attends the patient longings of Penelope, the humorous timidities of Laodamia, the tumultuous passion of Sappho. The poet has a modest garden, but he cultivates it intensively.

The writers in the *Heroides* are thus, after all, characters in elegy rather than tragedy and, perforce, characters in the kind of elegy that Ovid had made his own. The use of the elegiac metre is thus appropriate, if not inevitable. Wit, the poet's supporting virtue and his embarrassing vice, breaks forth in season and out. Briseis, he cannot forget, is heroine not only in the *Iliad,* but in Horace's ode to a young friend in love with a maid-servant. In Ovid's poem, humor plays delicately on the surface of pathos, — dangerous skating, which Horace

would have applauded. Laodamia is treated
with a freer hand; she well-nigh becomes matter for comedy. As her husband sails with the
army for Troy, she cautions him to beware of
Hector on the field. His campaigns are elsewhere.

In love, not war, a parfit, gentil knight, —
So let my dear one love, while others fight.

And let him be cautious in the landing! In the
thousand ships, be his the thousandth, and of
all on board, be he the last to leap ashore! All
this would turn the lament into burlesque, if
this were all. Again, as in *Briseis,* the undertone is pathos, with an approach to tragic
irony; for Protesilaus was to leap forth first,
not last, and fall by Hector's spear.

The strands of grave and gay fail to unite
in the *Heroides* when gayety brings us from
the heroic age plump into that of Augustus.
Tell-tale reminiscences of the *Amores* are all
too plentiful. Penelope apprehends from her
husband the dreadfully Ovidian reproach of
rusticity. Briseis slips from her tent quite in
the manner of Corinna eluding the concierge.
Phaedra has studied an advance-copy of the
Art of Love. The heroine of Euripides, to be

sure, is as adroit, and Hippolytus delivers a
kind of *Anti-Ovidius, sive de Arte non Amandi;*
but all this finesse is, in the play, caught up
into tragedy, with its deep questionings of divine justice and human fate. When, in the letter, Jove is displayed as the first Augustan and
critic of rusticity, illusion takes wings and the
atmosphere of the *Amores* is about us.

That ancient piety, doomed soon to die,
Lasted through Saturn's rustic dynasty.
Jove called things righteous if they pleasant be,
Wedded his sister and made morals free.

Ovid does not quite turn Phaedra's appeal into
comedy. Would that he had done so! He has
merely out-Euripidized Euripides.

The poems of the *Heroides,* despite their
artificialities, lapses in taste and the presence
of jocoseness where one looks for grief, are
alive today for the reason that Ovid has ac-
complished the chief purpose for which he
wrote them. We should regard them not as
unsuccessful attempts at tragic monologue, but
as thoroughly competent studies of woman's
moods. To Catullus and the other predecessors
of Ovid in love-elegy, woman is an unsolved
riddle. The poet can analyze his own emotions,

but back of them is the impenetrable CAUSE,
from which he moves uneasily away. Lesbia
is vividly a person because her worshipper is.
We can reason back, theologically, from effect
to cause, and have no doubt that she very
much exists. We know that she is beautiful
and passionate and wicked; she bites. But
what the inner workings of her soul are, Catullus cannot tell. He can get no farther than
sentio et excrucior. Tibullus and Propertius
are still less capable of an answer. We doubt
the reality even of their own feelings; their
mistresses fade into the background of literary
conventions; it matters not whether Plania was
really Hostia or who she was. Nor has Ovid,
in the *Amores,* much place for an analysis of
woman's moods. His chief amusement is in the
invention of his myth and in the ridicule of
the romantic lover who figures in it. But Ovid
is equipped by a superfeminine acuteness, —
I speak as a man — to understand women. He
is a member of that small coterie to which
Euripides before him, Chaucer, Boccaccio,
Shakespeare and Meredith after him had right
of entrance. It is in the *Heroides* that our poet
blithely embarks upon the great adventure:

Insano iuvat indulgere furori.

[23]

There are manifold types of woman and woman's moods in the poem, — wife, sister, step-mother, servant, shepherdess, queen, the trusting girl, the vengeful woman, the *ingénue* and the adept in passion and its art. The study of Phaedra will satisfy us better, if we look not for tragedy or even pathos, but for a searching analysis of a woman's longings, casuistries and wrongs. Ovid's Phaedra is less noble than the heroine of Euripides's play, but she is altogether as complex. In his portrayal of Dido, our poet subjects himself even more audaciously to comparison, and has been treated with general contumely and misunderstanding for his pains. Ovid is not correcting Virgil. He is picturing a different heroine, less queenly, more subtle. He would interpret the turnings and returnings of her emotions, like the colors on the changing sea, at the moment when, certain of her betrayal, she would send her sister to implore Aeneas for a short reprieve. It will not do merely to say that Ovid has replaced a heroine by a woman. No truer woman ever suffered than Virgil's Dido. But Ovid avoids tragedy; his Dido is a person of more humor, irony and common sense. She is in one mood, — when she speaks of her unborn

THE WORLD OF POETRY

child — more heroic, not less. She can be fairly blunt and brutal in showing her traitor the commercial advantage of settling in Carthage. Then in an instant she is a weak and loving woman, begging her life of him. Dryden declares that Virgil's portrayal of Dido must yield to the Myrrha, the Biblis, the Althaea of Ovid, who has "touched these tender strokes more delicately than Virgil could." [8]

Incidental to Ovid's plan is a certain depreciation of his own sex. There is material for a comic Aeneas in Dido's letter. He is fickle, rock-hearted, short-sighted, perjured, superstitious, ungallant and somewhat naïve; he thinks that after seven years of miscellaneous buffetings on the deep he is the darling of the gods. He owes his safety to her, not them; she saved him from a watery grave and gave him food and clothes. His eye is on the main chance and his great mission is the love of war for war's sake; he is bellicose but not heroic. Above all, — here *is* a slam at Virgil — he is fickle and feminine. *Varium et mutabile Aeneas!* So is Jason,

Mobilis Aesonides vernaque incertior aura

mobile più che il vento! Ovid has pointed the

[25]

way for Chaucer's *Legend of Good Women* and
partly depicted Meredith's egoist, — that is,
any man — who is as capricious as a woman
and who finds woman capricious chiefly because his logical processes operate less quickly.
Ovid damned Aeneas for all time and prevented some readers from understanding the
tragedy of the fourth *Aeneid*, which needs, and
displays, the suffering of the hero no less than
of the heroine. Ovid's Aeneas is the father of
a long line of villains, ridiculed by Jean de
Meun, by Chaucer, by Shakespeare, by Scarron and by Prior in his infamous couplet:

*Nor sing I Aeneas, who led by his mother
Got rid of one wife and went far for another.*

But Chaucer and Shakespeare, and Ovid, too,
are writing for a purpose, in which a tragic
Aeneas would be eminently out of place.

If we remove the *Heroides* from the realm
of tragedy to that of psychology, and allow
Ovid's wit a wider range than first appeared
appropriate, we shall better understand his
heroical letters and their writers. Nothing
would have amused him more than to see an
excess of seriousness imputed to them. When
Henry Esmond read Lady Castlewood his ver-

sified renderings of the *Epistles,* particularly
the strains in which Medea and Oenone call
after their false lovers, " she sighed and said
she thought that part of the verses most pleas-
ing." Thackeray had no small share of the
anima naturaliter Ovidiana, for he adds: " Indeed she would have chopped up the Dean,
her old father, in order to bring her husband
back again. But her beautiful Jason was gone,
as beautiful Jasons will go, and the poor enchantress had never a spell to keep him."

The Double Epistles

Ovid's friend Sabinus took up the cudgels
for the men, by composing answers, unhappily
not extant today, to several of the heroines'
letters; the heroes were allowed to explain
themselves. Ovid, acting on this hint, wrote
three double letters, message and reply, between Paris and Helen, Leander and Hero,
Acontius and Cydippe. It is strange that the
genuineness of these poems was debated so
long; if they are not from Ovid's pen, an
ignotus has beaten him at his own game.

The letter of Paris is a masterful application
of the precepts of the art of love. He begins

by declaring his passion. That is the whole
story; he loves her. But more, his love is di-
vinely enjoined. Appointed arbiter in the contest of the three goddesses, he favored Venus,
and Helen is the prize. He has come over the
seas for her. And when he saw her, — it seemed
the vision of Venus again. But is he worthy?
His lineage springs from Jove and his kingdom
is far wealthier than poor little Sparta. Poor
little Sparta? That was not well said. The land
that gave Helen birth is paradise. Yet, really,
such beauty needs transplanting to an even
fairer garden. And the women do dress well in
Troy; receptions are crowded with models of
the latest style; the very latest seems not yet
to have reached Sparta. Poor old Menelaus, he
ill appreciates his treasure. Oh the torture of
that banquet, to see him at her side! Paris
could but sigh, and gather from the lips of little
Hermione the kisses that her mother had left
there, and sound her handmaids, Clymene and
Aethra. Ah, if she would but yield to the Fates
and abandon the impossible contest between
virtue and beauty, — such beauty as hers!
Simple little Helen, — he will not call her rustic — not to see that the gods are on their side.
The laws of heredity can hardly create Puri-

tanism in the offspring of Leda and Jove. It is all arranged by her husband's stupid complaisance, his lack of any feeling for her. How lonely her couch must be! Her lover's is loneliness itself. He can offer her eternal fidelity and a right royal progress amidst the crowds of Troy. No harm in that, no prospect of calamity or war among the nations. Jason stole Medea from Colchis, and no Colchian war ensued. But suppose a war, is Paris not a champion? Is Hector not his brother? And should her beauty launch a thousand ships in a world-conflict, think what her fame would be throughout all time. Oh why not obey the gods and open her arms to the delights awaiting her!

Who would resist such rhetoric? Not Helen.

A little while she strove and much repented,
And whispering, " I will ne'er consent," consented.

Helen's answer is as delicately contrived as Paris's appeal; the opening lines tell the story:

" *Could I unread, oh Paris, what I read,*
  Chaste should I be, as chaste I once was bred.
  But as my eyes are stained by reading through,
  'Twere idle vengeance not to answer you."

This is surrender; the rest is apology. It is a long apology, with twists and turns, backings and fillings, defiance and remorse, and absolute capitulation. She begins in a blaze of indignation. The taunt of rusticity is the first to be answered. She admits that her looks do not suggest the Puritan. Her mood then softens to one of astonishment, and that to one of incredulity. How did he *dare?* Few wives are chaste, perhaps, but might she not be an exception? Heredity counts for little; she labors the point triumphantly, — Ovid's women are often victorious in skirmishes before the great defeat. Still, she owns that it is a minor argument. *Could* she consent, it would be only for love. She had noticed his doings at table; she dwells on them with a certain fondness, particularly the greedy look in the rascal's eyes. He would have made a fine lover, for some other woman, or for Helen, — at some other time. Why was he not among her early suitors? It is wrong, it is cruel to urge her now. The heart may yield, but duty opposes. And that contest of the goddesses, — a pretty myth indeed. To think that she, Helen of Troy, should be named by Venus as the prize. Preposterous! And yet it is a pretty compliment for Paris to pay.

After all, who knows? It were dangerous to
offend the gods. Perhaps, perhaps, she might
love, if she only knew the way. If someone
had only instructed her in *Ars Amandi!* If it
were done, then it were well if it were done
secretly. Of course Menelaus is away; really
it was rather ludicrous in him to bid her take
good care of Paris; all that she could say, to
keep from smiling, was " I will." Oh no, it
cannot be. How shameful to betray such confidence. And her fears, — possibly the cure for
rusticity would be compulsion. But what will
they think of her in that strange land? Will
she not be an outcast and a thing of scorn? It
is a fascinating prospect, though; what could
the Trojan styles be like? No, it is all false.
Jason made such promises to Medea. There is
something to apprehend from the wrathful goddesses whom Paris rejected. He is wrong about
the chances of war; there have been plenty of
battles over love. Paris, further, is hardly a
champion. He is born for love, not war. Let
Hector do the fighting, and he, — oh, he can
have her. Enough of words, Clymene and
Aethra will arrange the rest!

Incomparable audacity, the radiant attend-
ants of Helen of the *Iliad* degraded to the

circle of Corinna's maids! Bernard Shaw could
not shock us more. It were unforgivable, were
it not a logical conclusion from the Homeric
Helen's acts. Something like this happened in
Sparta. Ovid is thinking out ancient history,
the part that the historians do not record.
Following Euripides, once more, he has transformed heroic lovers, playthings of the gods,
into human beings, and solved a human problem in a perfect work of art. No less perfect
in art and reality are the letters of Acontius to
Cydippe and the little girl's reply. If apology
or " serious relief " is demanded after Helen's
surrender, it is here. The actors in this little
drama are boy and girl; their love is pure and
tender. Simplicity is not always rustic. Acontius has an untaught art of love unerringly
effective. Cydippe does not submit without a
course of moods, reproach and tantalizing ridicule among them, as wealthy, in their way, as
those of Helen. These four poems, and the
moonlit lines describing Leander's swim, would
put Ovid in the front rank of poets, had he
written nothing more.

iii. THE ART OF LOVE

Avyseth yow and putte me out of blame;
And eek men shal nat make ernest of game. CHAUCER

Ah Rustick, ruder than Gothick! CONGREVE

Scis vetus hoc iuveni lusum mihi carmen et istos
    Ut non laudandos sic tamen esse iocos. OVID

After the experiences recorded in the *Amores*,
it is small wonder that our poet felt himself
an expert in the ways of love. He now writes,
therefore, what is in form a didactic poem,
one that the historian of literature must put
on the same shelf with Virgil's *Georgics* and
the *De Rerum Natura* of Lucretius. As the
subject of the new poem is still fit matter for
elegy, Ovid makes no change in his metre.
Had he commenced in the heroic verse that
Virgil and Lucretius had employed, Cupid
would have smiled again, as the beginning of
the *Amores* pictures him, and stolen away a
foot from every line.

The *Art of Love* was preceded by a little
work which must have created some excitement
among Roman beauties, on the *Art of Cosmetic* (*De Medicamine Faciei*). Only a fragment of this poem is preserved. It opens with

a panegyric on culture, of which agriculture was the only sort appreciated in primitive days.

When Tatius ruled, the buxom Sabine dame,
For feats of spinning known to rustic fame,
With country dainties piled the groaning shelf
And dressed her corn-land better than herself.

But these Mid-Victorian virtues are outgrown. The rising generation in Rome, as possibly in any age, has changed all that.

For tender mothers bear us tender girls
Who dress in gold and crimp their fragrant curls,
Or cut them off, or wave or bang or part,
And gain complexions with a stroke of art.

O matre molli filia mollior! Ovid has found his clientèle and shown himself a connoisseur. Perhaps he was in collusion with the beauty-shops of his time. His lines have the ring of metrical advertisement, like Andrew Lang's poem on " Matrimony." At all events, Ovid's scholarship is profound; he doubtless flowed on for many more verses than those that chance has transmitted to us.

The *Art of Love* is no less scholarly. The title *Ars Amatoria* suggests not merely a course in intrigue, but a text-book of the subject, a companion-volume to an *ars grammatica* or an *ars rhetorica*. The poem opens with a panegyric on Art, which is needed in all the walks of life. The skipper needs it on the deep, the driver needs it in his speeding car, the lover needs it above all. " Ce sont des règles," explains Molière's heroine to her rustic uncle, " dont en bonne galanterie on ne saurait dispenser." It is no light task for the poet to instruct Cupid; still, he is a boy after all. So, then, for the Invocation, — except that none is necessary. The poet has been blessed with no special inspiration from the Muses; his subject is true! It is also highly moral; for he sings only of love sanctioned by the law. So, matrons, long of skirt and high of brow, avaunt! There is nothing that concerns you here. This is the demi-monde with its battles of love where all is fair. The reader breathes a sigh of relief; nothing to shock us here, as in the *Amores!*

The poet proceeds to a formal division of his subject-matter: A. How to Find Her; B. How to Win Her; C. How to Keep Her. Nothing could be more comprehensive. The first article can best be followed by an expert in topography; for to show just where the willing

maiden may be met, Ovid takes us all over
Rome, along colonnades, to the temples, especially of the Oriental and liberal divinities,
to the ancient forum and the fora lately added,
to the theatre, — ah, there's fine hunting-
ground!

As ants to grain and bees to flowers hie,
To scenic pictures do our damsels fly.

A double reason brings them:

To see they come, and come they to be seen.

All praise to Romulus, founder of Rome and
first patron of the stage! The poet diverts us
into the tale of the stolen Sabines, so brilliantly
and rapidly told, that, as in a simile of Homer's,
we are transported from the main scene of
action into a different world which is its own
excuse for existence.

You, Romulus, knew how your men to pay.
Grant me such wage and I'll enlist today,

ends the poet. He would have relished the
by-scene of a worthy Sabine house-holder, as
Xavier de Maistre pictures him, who after the
event exclaims in despair: "Dieux immortels!

[36]

Pourquoi n'ai j' point amené ma femme à la
fête!" [9]

So much for Where to Find Her. Now, How
to Win Her. Precepts can guide us. As Lucretius based his philosophy of the universe
on axioms, beginning with the law of *nihil ex
nihilo,* so Ovid starts blithely with a kind of
omnia ex omnibus. For, first and foremost, no
woman is invulnerable; " *omnes posse capi.*"
Woman seems more modest because man is a
less skilful dissembler.

Were it the mode our fair ones not to woo,
You'd find your fair one would importune you.

Other precepts follow thick and fast. Study
her entourage, her social ego, and make yourself a favorite with her personnel. Study the
times and seasons, as Hesiod's farmer minded
days as well as works. Intertwined with this
theme is one on the art of giving, that is, of
giving as little as possible. Her birthday is an
unlucky time for a visit; choose a day of National Mourning, when no games are going on.
Ah me, that's something hard to find. Some
girls contrive to have a year of birthdays. Pave
the way with a letter in the proper style. A
liberal education is of some use after all; it

teaches the art of persuasion. But do not treat your mistress to an oration. Avoid big words; be vivid, dramatic, convincing. If she makes no answer, try again. All things come in time.

Penelope's own self in time you'll win!
Troy long resisted, but at last gave in.

Penelope seems an inappropriate example. Was she not a matron? The poet seems to have forgotten the subject of this work. He hastens to give more precepts. Learn how to dance attendance on her; learn how to dress. Cultivate simplicity and a certain sweet disorder which maidens like. But do not be too Bohemian; trim your nails and forget not to shave. Do not wear sloppy sandals and keep your toga free from spots.

The temperance question! Learn to drink with art. This is a rich subject, in which various precepts are involved, as in the interweaving of the themes of a symphony. It needs an invocation to Bacchus, and the rehearsal of his wooing of Ariadne, a rollicking tale, with rollicking verse to describe the manly attempts of the drunken Silenus to keep pace with the Maenads, — at last he falls off his donkey. The god drives up in his tiger-cart to comfort

[38]

the heroine, and courteously descends, lest the tigers frighten her, — courtesy is a golden maxim for Ovid's gallant. The moral is: use the god's gift of wine to win your Ariadne, but do not let it go to your head. Write messages on the table in wine for her to see, and look unspeakable things at her. Display the utmost courtesy to the husband, — *is* it husband? *Vir* is the word; perhaps it merely means lover; the situation is getting a bit confused. At any rate, give him the first chance at the bowl. Offer him your wreath of flowers. In the concert of talk, play second fiddle to him. Study your accomplishments. Sing if you can; if your arms are graceful, dance eurythmically. Pretended inebriation is a help; you can do things then for which you seem not responsible. That is the time to seek her side and lavish compliments however absurd.

> *She'll swallow all. No girl, however plain,*
> *Dislikes her looks or thinks her beaux insane.*

Jean de Meun applied this universal truth to his town times with a sly satire worthy of his master.[10]

> *Car il n'est fame, tant soit bone,*
> *Vielle ou jone, mondaine ou none,*

Ne si religieuse dame,
Tant soit chaste de cors et d'ame,
Se l'en va sa biauté loant,
Qui ne se délite en oant.

The precepts on wine and its use in the first approach to your mistress's favor lead easily to the next, which prescribes the technique of promises and false oaths. Perjury is generally detestable. Religion and its obligations are a vital need. But when it comes to women, *fallite fallentes;* deceive your deceivers; do unto them as they do unto you. Some righteous indignation is displayed in the treatment of this theme. Along with oaths and promises, tears will be found useful, and there are ways of producing them at will. Kisses are effective; apply them boldly. Maidens like vigorous action. Do not wait for them to begin. The poet caps his argument with a supreme example:

Jove wooed the heroines on bended knee.
No maid corrupted him with amorous plea.

Iuppiter locutus est; causa finita est. The main argument of the first book is done, but the poet adds an epilogue. He was about to conclude, when he bethought him of the diversity of woman's nature. Doubtless the reader will find that none of the instructions will fit his case. Some fish are caught with a hook and some with a drag-net. The lover should always be on the move, always adaptive, always ready for the sudden turn.

Act like the nimble Proteus. Turn your coat,
Changing to water, tree, boar, lion or to goat!

The life of the Ovidian lover is a perpetual, and sometimes humiliating, metamorphosis.

The reader will assume that the argument of the second book, " How to Keep Her," is carried out with similar thoroughness. In this difficult undertaking, the gallant has many comic parts to play. He must postpone all his business at his lady's call. If she is in the country he must speed thither in his fastest car. If no chariot is his, let him foot it briskly. No running slave in comedy can be brisker, or more ludicrous than he. All Rome will see him carrying her parasol — a menial task in those days. He will often have to thread his way on a pitch-dark night through sudden down-pours, or sleep on the ice-cold sill. When the front portal is barred, he will climb up by a window or steal in at the sky-light.

One consolation there is; this sturdy disci-

pline is not for the wealthy lover; he needs it
not. Ovid preaches to the poor. The rich barbarian needs no passport; the poet's passport
rarely gets him by the door. There is, to be
sure, a small, very small, coterie of blue-
stockings:

Some girls have culture, but they're mighty few.
Some want to get it, — or they think they do.

Here is where the poet-lover has a chance, a
slim one, with his

Rimes jolietes,
Motez, fabliaus, ou chançonetes.[11]

In most houses, however, Homer himself, at-
tended by all nine Muses, will be shown the
door.

For all its naughtiness, the poem is not without its ethical lessons. The poet constructs a
kind of Mirror of the Chivalrous Lover, which
is the counterpart, and in many respects, the
model, of the Mediaeval Knightly Code, as we
see it in the *Romance of the Rose*. Patience
and courtesy are the cardinal virtues, anger
and pride the deadly sins. The lover should
cultivate a pleasant temper. He must study his

[42]

lady's desires and fit his mood to hers. Laugh
with her, cry with her, yield to her opinions.
Let her beat at games; escort her to receptions,
whither you may not care to go. Let her man-
age, or think she does. Learn to pay her
compliments with a straight face. Admire her
dresses, each for its own virtue; note the
changes in her art of arranging her hair.

She parts her hair; then praise the comely line.
She crimps it; call those twisted locks divine.

Serve as her doctor when she is ill. Do every-
thing for her, — except administering the medicine; let your rival do that. Give her defects
the names of proximate virtues; say " slender "
for " skinny," " trim " for " puny," " buxom "
for " stout." It is an easy art, which Plato and
Horace had prescribed before Ovid and the
heroines of Molière and Congreve practised
after him. Prior sums it up in a neat couplet,
since become a proverb:

Be to her virtues very kind,
Be to her faults a little blind.[12]

Finally, — for Ovid's precepts always are subject to a sudden turn, — it may be well to

arouse your darling's jealousy and her temper
now and then. Blessings on the *amantium irae,*
if they all the more endear:

Oh four times blest and blest times infinite
Is he who wounds his love and stirs her spite.
When gossip simmers and she, loath to hear,
Losing all voice and color, faints in fear,
May I be he whose locks she madly tears!
May I be he whose cheek her nail-prints bears!
At whom she looks with tearful little eyes,
Sans whom she cannot live, though hard she tries.

The last book of the poem is the most brilliant, if anything can be more brilliant than the
first two; in other words, the poet's climax is
sustained. With a complete *volte-face,* Ovid
now deserts his sex and instructs the maiden
how to win a lover and how to keep him. He
begins with a " Legend of Good Women," ex-
actly on Chaucer's plan and that of Jean de
Meun before him. It is accompanied by the
same ruthless exhibition of man's shiftiness
that we saw in the *Heroides.* " Deceive your
deceivers!" That maxim is passed on, with a
courteous bow, to the fair. Whether Ovid's
precepts are sound is not for a mere man to
judge. On the attractiveness of mourning ap-

parel, on the danger of getting mad at cards, on the use of the mirror as a cure for temper, on the practice of various modes of hand-writing for various lovers, on the advisability of completing one's toilet before leaving the house, lest, as the poet puts it, "you show yourself a work of art in the making," — on these and many other matters some *docta puella* should tell us whether Ovid has hit the mark.

The maidens to whom the poet gives counsel are, as ever, those of the lower world. He had intended a brief digression on the way for wives to elude their shrewd husbands and wakeful porters. No, no! Rather he had meant to pass that topic by. But he will add a suggestion for the reform of the home. If the wife would arouse her husband's love, let her make love less easy for him. Shut him out! Let him hear the concierge say gruffly, as he slams the door in his face, "*Non potes!*" "No you don't!" With his sense of adventure spurred, the master of the house can then climb in at my Lady's window.

Such is Ovid's *Art of Love*, being, as a French critic pithily observes,[13] "*l'art d'aimer sans amour*," the work of one who can apostrophize himself in Chaucer's words:

*And peynest thee to preyse (Love's) art,
Although thou haddest never part.*[14]

Ovid's poem is a monument of art, of chis-
elled verses with the sparkle of diamonds. It
is a monument of wit and delicate travesty,
prompted by deviltry and restrained by no re-
luctance to shock. The poet spares none of the
mysteries of sex. He shrinks from nothing. But
it is not prurience or morbidity but audacity
to the point of blasphemy that leads him to
disclose with a reckless frankness what in all
decency should be left unsung. Matrons are
warned off the field, but by irony and innuendo
we are constantly made aware that the world
of intrigue portrayed in the *Art of Love* differs
not at all from that in the *Amores*. Nor does
the earlier work fail to contain pieces quite as
impossible for a writer today as the notorious
grand finales in the *Art of Love*. If writing of
this sort deserved exile, Ovid should have been
banished in his early twenties.

Towards the close of the poem, Ovid illus-
trates the evils of jealousy by the story of
Cephalus and Procris. The young huntsman,
Cephalus, tired after the chase, would rest in
a grove and sing the praise of Aura, the breeze,
who came to refresh him. Procris, minded of

Aurora, the Dawn - goddess, who had once
stolen him from her, goes in search of him. He
hears a rustling in the bushes, and thinking
that some creature of the woods is coming
towards him, shoots an arrow thither. He
rushes into the thicket and finds that he has
slain his wife. The story is told in lines of
liquid grace, and an exquisite pathos not far
removed from tragedy. This is the moment of
serious relief in Ovid's dare-devil comedy. It
is his apology, much needed, for his transgressions, proclaimed with clearness for those who
have ears to hear.

When all is said, the *Art of Love* cannot
permanently harm a reader who, equipped with
a sense of humor, finds something in the poem
besides a manual of seduction. Landor, in the
imaginary conversation which he devises for
Tibullus and Messala, makes the latter re-
mark:

" Before I left Ovidius — he read to me the
commencement of some amatory pieces, at
which if I smiled, it was in courtesy, not ap-
probation."

Really, there is another reason for which Messala might have smiled.

iv. THE REMEDIES OF LOVE

I find the Medicine worse than the Malady.
BEAUMONT AND FLETCHER

Quid faciam? Monitis sum minor ipse meis.
OVID

The gossips at Rome had been busy with the *Art of Love*. An apology seemed appropriate, and Ovid proceeded cheerfully to recant. He lost no time in so doing. An allusion to the Parthian expedition as still under way fixes the date of the *Remedia,* like that of the *Art of Love,* between 1 B.C. and 1 A.D. Both works, therefore, were done within the space of two years. It is a remarkable achievement, for though Ovid composed with ease, he must have spent some time in planning his intricate structures, in elaborating his parodies and audacities as fast as they occurred to his lively imagination, and in polishing his first drafts of verse into the peerless art of its finished form.

The apology, we find somewhat to our surprise, is not to us but to Cupid. Cupid scents a battle and the poet reassures him that his object is not to annihilate love, — in fact he himself is laboring with a bad attack at the moment — but only in case some desperate lover is on the point of suicide, to suggest a few precepts that may restore his sanity. Cupid, mollified, puts up his arrows and gives the work his *Imprimatur*. So Dr. Ovid, in the manner of the street-preacher of his day, gathers youths and maidens about him, to listen to his message of healing. Come ere it be too late! Could Phyllis and Dido and even unhappy Pasiphaë have consulted the doctor, their lives would have been models of felicity and common sense. Could Helen have come in time, this same physician would have prevented the Trojan War! With an invocation to Phoebus the Healer, he writes out his prescriptions.

Begin the cure at once, that is, tomorrow. Yet even if the disease is well established, call in the doctor; it may not be too late. Perhaps he will advise that the fever run its course; that is well in the more violent cases. Be neither too fast nor too slow; watch for the psychological moment! Surely such admonition is safe, sane and scientific. We are disposed to trust this expert. Now for the specific cures. The first and most fatal obstacle to recovery is too much leisure. So get to work! Go into politics or law or enlist for service over seas against the Parthians. Work is the best anti-

dote for love. Aegisthus was not wholly to
blame for his offence. He was a slacker, true,
and had not joined the troops, but it was just
because Argos was deserted that he devoted his
attention to Agamemnon's wife; there was
nothing else to do! Perhaps your plan for in-
dustry may look towards the country. How
pleasant to see the cattle winding slowly over
the lea, to see trees laden with fruit and sheep
with wool, and, above all, to set out plants with
your own hands. The poet praises country life,
divini gloria ruris, as enthusiastically as Virgil
does in the *Georgics* or Horace in his epode,
with the underlying strain of light travesty conspicuous in the latter poem. But, our physician
adds, do not get a country-place too near to
Rome. Travel abroad. This is bitter medicine,
but efficacious, and far safer than the magic
potion, which he never recommends. In case
the patient cannot get away from town and
can find no engrossing occupation there, he
should apply a psycho-analytical treatment.
Make a list of your darling's imperfections and
rehearse this catalogue constantly.

The more she grabs, the less she is content.
Good-bye, small house, I cannot pay the rent!

She swore me oaths and broke whate'er she swore.
All night I've waited at the fast-barred door.
She's tired of me. With me intrigue were sin;
My vulgar rival, with the cash, gets in!

An advanced form of this method is the opposite of the principle laid down in the *Art of Love* that the gallant should rename his mistress's defects as though they were virtues; now he should rename her virtues as though they were defects.

To ills deflect her virtues, if you can,
And cheat your judgment by this subtle plan.
Obese the buxom, black the brunette call,
And swear the slender has no flesh at all.
Call pert the maiden who is not straight-laced,
And rustic call her, if, perchance, she's chaste.

Really, this cure is so complex that were the last line quoted by itself, many an expert might fancy that it was part of the *Art of Love* and not of the *Remedies*.

Thus far, the lover has directed his main attention to himself. But he should also study his mistress and plan a new course of action in his dealings with her. In brief, make her display her imperfections. If she has no voice, urge her to sing. If she is gawky, set her to

[51]

dancing. If her speech is distinguished mainly by bad grammar, engage her in lengthy conversations. If her teeth are uncomely, tell her funny stories; if her eyes tend to be bleary, move her to weeping by some tragic tale. Above all, pay an early morning call, before she has had time to manufacture a complexion and array herself in her jewels.

By gems we're captured and the dresser's art;
A girl's own person is her smallest part.

If the lover meets with no success in these and other attempts, some of them pretty desperate, let him turn his attention elsewhere. Let fire drive out fire! If he needs instructions in selecting a new mistress, the doctor can take down his standard work on the *Art of Love,* temporarily put on the shelf, and refer him to Part I, Chapter I, on "How to Find Her." *Fas est et ab hoste doceri!* This, then, may be the best way:

To quench the thirst that hath your stomach fired
Drink from mid-stream until your thirst hath tired.

The poet now comes, with a special invocation, to the second main division of his remedies. It corresponds to the section on " How

to Keep Her " in the *Art of Love*. It is now
" How to Keep Her Lost." Again there are
psychological precepts; again the gallant is instructed in the treatment of his former darling.
He should court the crowd, avoid solitude, but
likewise avoid contagious society. Particularly,
he must never protest that all is over. Hate her
not; hate and love are desperately contiguous.
Do not bring suit to recover your presents. Be
well prepared for a sudden meeting with her
again. Wear slouchy clothes. Turn a deaf ear
to her flattery and her tears. Above all, do not
argue with her the justice of your case; do not
give her a chance to argue. Burn her letters
and her pictures; avoid reminiscential scenes.
Lose all your money, if you can. Go not to the
theatre. Read no poetry of the softer sort;
never open your copy of Sappho or Tibullus.

Who can read Gallus and stay cool of heart?
My poems, too, have something of that art!

This were impartiality itself, for the physician
to warn the patient from his publications, —
were there not another class of patients, who
would find something of an advertisement here.

The treatment of your rival is the hardest
part of the cure. Do not think of him, or, if

you can, think of him as non-existing! When you can stand his presence, when you can kiss him, then you are cured. That is the acid test of convalescence, that and the ability to walk past your mistress's front door. Incidentally, cultivate a proper diet. Eat rue and other brain food. As to wine:

> *Drink not at all, or drink to drown your woe.*
> *'Tis dangerous in the middle course to go.*

So end the *Remedia*. The critics who expected a recantation perhaps have found this remedy indistinguishable from the disease. Curiously, though Ovid's patients whom he gathered about him at the beginning of his discourse included maidens as well as men, the precepts are all for the latter. Maidens can take care of themselves.

2. The Poet of Transformations

METAMORPHOSES

Like as the waves make towards the pebbled shore,
So do our minutes hasten to their end;
Each changing place with that which goes before,
In sequent toil all forward do contend.

. . . .

No, Time, thou shalt not boast that I do change. . . .
Thy registers and thee I both defy,
Not wondering at the present nor the past.

SHAKESPEARE

Sed ut unda impellitur unda,
Urgueturque eadem veniens urguetque priorem;
Tempora sic fugiunt pariter, pariterque sequuntur.

. . . .

Animus tamen omnia vincit.

OVID

THE higher theme which Ovid prophesied at
the end of his *Amores* had found a partial expression in his tragedy *Medea* and in the invention of heroines' love-letters. His youthful
impulse to epic, which had shattered on the
rocks of a conventional subject, still moved
him, and though the reader of Ovid's love-
poetry might gasp at the suggestion that it
would lead easily and naturally into epic, such
is the case. It may also seem strange that Ovid
should turn to mythology for a theme; he had
treated the ancient legends as the invention of
lying bards. Still, he could tell a metamorphosis or two himself, if occasion required. The
Ovidian lover can narrate a whole series of
myths to the swollen stream that bars the way
to his mistress. Myths of divine amours are
useful as " ensamples olde;" the gallant is
most learned in quoting such scripture for his

[55]

purpose. With each succeeding work, Ovid's facility in narrative increased. In the *Art of Love,* the brilliant rapidity of the incidental tales could hardly be surpassed. It is not surprising that the poet wished to try his wings in a longer flight through the same realm. The spirit of metamorphosis, furthermore, was ingrained in his nature. He relished nothing better than to set forth a mood or a situation with utter seriousness and then blithely to present the exact opposite. Shifts, set-backs, disappointments, metamorphoses, are the essence of life in his world of amorous adventure. It is also a little world of myth, with Corinna at its centre. Ovid had hugely enjoyed the rôle of creator; he is at once properly sceptical of poets' lies and confident of his own power to turn the chaos of brute fact into the cosmos of poetic reality. He had come to his own in an epic on metamorphosis.

It is unfortunate that none of the ancient poems on metamorphosis written before Ovid's time has come down to us in its complete form. Various writers had been fascinated with the theme. Among the Greeks are Nicander and " Boeus " in the Hellenistic age; among the Romans is Aemilius Macer, whose poem on the transformations of humans into birds Ovid had heard from the lips of the composer. Could we today read these and other such works entire, we should doubtless learn much about Ovid's procedure and his originality. Even now it is safe to say that no such metamorphoses as his had ever been told before.

The backbone of Ovid's narrative is chronology. He professes to record the complete history of metamorphosis, as Dryden puts it,

Deduc'd from Nature's birth to Caesar's times.

This plan gives at once the full sweep of epic and, as Augustan epic might demand, allows for the tucking in of a bit of panegyric. Nicander's arrangement, so far as we can fathom, was geographical; but Ovid found small promise of climax in a Baedeker. He likewise is not attracted by the traditional arrangement followed in handbooks of mythology, like that of Apollodorus. The latter starts out with chronology, but interrupts his plan almost at once. He finds himself tracing the history of various mythological families and has constantly to begin again. Jupiter is perpetually interfering; what can the genealogist do with one who becomes his own grandfather? The result is a hodge-podge, a "Who's Who Among the Gods," without an index.

Ovid is not embarrassed with so inclusive a plan. Not intending a *Summa Mythologiae,* he can more neatly present the semblance of a history and keep his narrative alive. Though a sober Apollodorus would find him dreadfully anachronistic at times, he covers such transgressions with a veil of illusion, and never allows the delight of the reader to turn to criticism. The number of myths that he manages to tell in the rolling course of universal metamorphosis is amazing. As he proceeded with his work, he was constantly occupied with the amusing problem of weaving into the texture of metamorphosis stories that had nothing to do with it. For example, the tale of Ceres and Proserpine lies, we should imagine, outside his domain, but in virtue of its setting and the tales of magical transformation told by the way and at the end, the atmosphere of metamorphosis is undisturbed. In this way, Ovid both preserves his original design and contrives, after all, a lexicon of the myths, — the Golden Legend of antiquity. The latest editor of Apollodorus, no mean authority on myths,[15] admires our poet not only for his exuberant fancy but for his learning and his fidelity to his sources. Ovid has beaten Apollodorus at his own game.

Ovid's predecessors in poems on metamorphosis had secured contrast and variety by infusing large amounts of amatory material into their narrative. Our poet was not slow to comply with such authority. He could also adopt the epic poet's familiar device of transporting the action to Olympus now and then. But what an Olympus it is! His first metamorphoses, — the evolution of the world from chaos, the course of the ages from gold to iron, the battle of the hosts of light and darkness — are told in stately and imaginative verse; it is the longest passage of uninterrupted sobriety that Ovid has given us thus far. With Jove, the curtain rises for another scene. We are introduced to a thoroughly Augustan heaven, where plebeian deities occupy the less desirable quarters and the upper classes reside in what the poet calls the *Palatine of the Sky*, with the Milky Way, the celestial Fifth Avenue, or "Watlinge strete," leading up to their mansions. Jupiter, incensed at the impiety of Lycaon, decides to destroy mankind with his thunderbolts, — but no, the fire might spread and ignite Olympus. A flood would be safer. As the waters cover the earth, the tone of the narrative becomes sober once more; the verses flow with liquid smoothness, and now sparkle again with a light humor, when the poet imagines some of the consequences of the flood, — the boatman gathering in fishes from the tree-tops, the nymphs of the sea, suddenly finding their domain augmented by houses and towns, the dolphins butting against tree-trunks as they swim about. Now comes a touch of pathos, as the bird after long search for dry land

On wearied pinions drops into the sea.

After history starts again with the rock-born race of mortals, the jovial deities reappear. Apollo, in the manner of the pastoral swain, woos Daphne on the run. Jove is smitten with the charms of Io, hides her beneath a cloud from the jealous eye of Juno, who melts the cloud, — when, presto! Io has been transformed into a heifer. Pan's sweetheart is the nymph Syrinx, turned to a reed as the enamoured deity is about to embrace her. Mercury tells this story so soothingly, that Argus, set by Juno to guard the suspicious heifer, drops asleep and is promptly put to death. Io begins her long wanderings, which end in Egypt with her new and glorious metamorphosis into a goddess. Her boy Epaphus, jesting with his friend Phaëthon, denies the latter's claim to be the offspring of the Sun. Phaëthon runs to his mother, Clymene, who reassures him and bids him learn the truth for himself from his father.

> He *heard her joyfully and bounded forth*
> *Past Aethiopia and the Indians' land*
> *That lies beneath the stars. Then up the sky*
> He *mounted dauntless to his sire's realm.*

We are at the end of the first book, with promise of some excitement in the continuation of the tale, — a device appreciated by Ovid long before the invention of the serial novel.

It were ungracious to notice all the adventures of the amorous gods who figure in Ovid's poem. Never was Aristotle's dictum better justified that the persons of comedy are worse than those in every-day life. Jupiter is easily the protagonist, smitten with each fair face and thwarted by Nemesis in the form of Juno. But nothing daunts him. He espies the beautiful huntress Callisto and exclaims:

> My *spouse will know not of these stolen sweets,*
> *Or, if she know, the sweets are worth the scolding.*

Phoebus and Mercury are worthy seconds to
Jove. The messenger of the gods, who in this
poem is invariably sent on some errand of
gallantry, has many a chance to pick a damsel
for himself. Fresh from his theft of Apollo's
cattle, he takes his aerial way over Athens at
the moment when the basket-bearing maidens
are winding up the Acropolis in solemn proces-
sion to pay homage to the virgin goddess's
shrine. Mercury likes the sight. He wheels
round and round in the air, like a greedy kite
above the entrails at a sacrifice; this is not a
reverent comparison. Old Sol enters the field
for a display of epic valor, — ἀριστεία, Homer
would call it, ἐρωτεία is perhaps the word —
and he is quadruply victorious. The only innocent among the divinities is the virgin huntress.
When Callisto rejoins Diana's troop after her
adventure with Jove,

Silent she blushed with shame for virtue gone.
Were Dian not a virgin, she had seen
A thousand proofs of guilt. The nymphs, 'tis said,
Observed them.[16]

So runs this irreverent comedy for five books,
alternating with Phaëthon's mad race in the
chariot of the Sun, the founding of Thebes by

the dragon-slayer Cadmus, the triumph of the Wine-God, the rescue of a princess by the knightly Perseus, and his boastful story of his exploits that leads to a free and mock-heroic fight over the cups, till Perseus flashes the Gorgon's head at his assailants and turns them into statues. At the beginning of the sixth book, the escapades of the gods culminate in the story of Arachne, who blasphemously invites Minerva to a contest in spinning and covers her web with the most scandalous amours of the gods. It is the grand finale of Ovid's *Divine Comedy*. Arachne is promptly turned into a spider; what condign metamorphosis should be decreed to the poet, Diana might decide. He deserves a prize for ridiculing an outworn theology with a fine pungency beside which Lucian's diatribes seem primitive and tame.

Though the gods are off the stage, heroes are given their share of burlesque, particularly when they figure in the hunt of the Calydonian boar. One trips over a stump, one hides in the background, Nestor escapes the beast by performing a pole-vault into a tree, and the honor of drawing the first blood falls to a woman. The action is also diversified by innumerable

stories of love. There is the wild and vengeful
love of the witch Medea, the unfilial love
of Scylla for her father's foe, the all-too-filial
love of Myrrha for her father, the chivalrous
love of Meleager for Atalanta, the incestuous
love of Byblis for her brother, the love of the
young Centaur for his bride, the love of Narcissus, — most complicated case of all — for himself. What next? Why, the love of Cephalus
for his wife, a tragic story deep and true, giving "serious relief" amidst these distressing
amorosities. Ovid had used it for this purpose
in the *Art of Love*. He tells it again, and he
tells it even better. Ovid reveals his inner
depths of reverence when he writes:

> I *fondly dwell, oh son of Aeacus,*
> O*n those blest days of wedlock new,*
> T*hen when we each to each were all in all.*[17]

Ovid is not responsible for all of his stories
of unhallowed love. He is following an unpleasant tradition set by his Greek predecessors, who
had gone to greater lengths than he. Ovid has
selected and refined. He is not the victim of
morbid curiosity; he uses pathological matter
for different effects. He begins the tale of Byblis with a shiver of horror, and sustains tragic

feeling to the end. In the story of Myrrha, pathos is mingled recklessly with burlesque. You cannot take that sort of thing seriously twice! But Centaur-love he treats without a flicker of burlesque. The beauty of Cyllara, half-brute though she is, is set forth in lines of epic dignity. If we smile at her feminine propensity

> *On her left shoulder or her side to hang*
> *Becoming beast-skins in the latest style,*[18]

it is no smile of derision, and it changes to pity and sorrow when the lovers meet their death. Will the love of the half-brute Polyphemus be treated by our poet in the same fashion? Hardly. This most uncouth swain is hero in an entertaining travesty of the pastoral. He combs his locks with a rake and performs a serenade to his Galatea on a Pan's pipe of an hundred reeds, a veritable church-organ; the serenade is arranged elaborately into strophes and antistrophes and is set to loud music with ponderous rhymes and grating dissonance.

Our poet's love of variety is no less manifest in the other strands of which the story is woven. Every book has its contrasts of grave and gay, and these elements are never mixed in the same proportion or occupy the same places in a book. For variety's sake, one whole book is devoted to love, and the songs are by one singer, Orpheus, who reveals the kind of songs to which the oaks gave ear, — no wonder that the Maenads tore him to bits! Devices for introducing the stories are invented with an apparently inexhaustible ease. They are narrated as the pieces rendered in a contest in song or described in the works of contestants in weaving; they form after-dinner speeches, or the tales that soldiers swap; they are parts of the experiences of long-separated friends, told to each other as they meet again; they are parts of women's gossip, — no better narrator of the deeds of the infant Hercules than Alcmene, his mother, and no better auditor than Iole, his latest love. Glaucus woos his maiden with the story of his own metamorphosis; Vertumnus assumes a metamorphosis in wooing his. A brilliant device is the setting of the amorous stories of the daughters of Minyas in an atmosphere of horror; while all Thebes celebrates the rites of the new god of the vine, they blasphemously stay at home and as they spin, blasphemously regale themselves with scandal; vengeance is gathering for them, and at the return of the god, the spinsters' woof grows into the ivy and the vine that they had despised; the maidens themselves turn into chattering bats. Boccaccio, helped doubtless by Ovid's art, effects a similar contrast between the gay tales of the *Decamerone* and their grewsome occasion.

As we glide along the varied course of Ovid's story, with changes in moods and colors, changes in the music of the verse, changes in the settings, changes in the actors at the end of the tale, we become gradually aware that the spirit of the poem is constantly changing as it moves. It starts as epic and is epic throughout. It has not the nobility of Virgil's poem, which only Milton among the countless imitators of Virgil could reproduce. Ovid, avoiding what he knew was impossible for him, invented what was impossible for Virgil, an epic that with the easy, romantic flow of the *Odyssey,* takes on different colors in its course. Now it seems comedy, now elegy, now pastoral. Now it becomes a hymn, now tragedy. Now the poet, with some daring, shifts the scene to the rostra, where Ajax and Ulysses debate the right to wear the armour of the slain Achilles. Ovid lavishes on this debate his full store of rhetori-

cal subtleties and psychological observation. It
is drama of a high order and oratory that
Cicero might envy; it also impressed Landor,
a critic hard to please, as more epic than the
Aeneid. Didactic poetry in the vein of Lucretius appears in the first book of the poem and
in the last. Panegyric is sounded, not too
loudly, at the beginning and again at the end.
Every book in the poem is different, and every
one the same, like the faces of the nymphs
whose images Vulcan wrought in the palace of
the Sun,

> *Like and unlike, as sister-nymphs beseems.*

In adjusting his narrative, Ovid has many
nice problems to solve, many impossibilities
to make real by the art of illusion. Roughly
speaking, the poem falls into three parts. The
action is first in the world of the gods, then in
that of the heroes, and lastly in that of men.
It is the time-honored division of Pindar's ode,
and Horace's:

τίνα θεόν, τίν' ἥρωα, τίνα δ'ἄνδρα κελαδήσομεν.

But these divisions shade into one another and
each contains matter that belongs elsewhere.
" Pyramus and Thisbe " is a love-story of the

Hellenistic age, but it is told by the daughters of Minyas in the mythical days of Pentheus of Thebes. Still, it might have been familiar before the flood. Who cares? It does not disturb the reader's sense of the descending sweep of time. The moment he may feel that he is floating about in a timeless realm of myth, the poet, with a magic touch, attaches the myth to history, as when Apollo, flying away after his victory over Pan, sees Laomedon far beneath him, building the walls of Troy. We know where we are and what is coming; the Trojan War is not far away. When it comes, Ovid takes care not to enter the lists against either Homer or Virgil. He tells what metamorphoses he can at the beginning, and narrates the death of Achilles at the end. The intervening stretch of time must be wiped out. With an amusing sort of illusion, he manages to slide o'er full nine years

>   *and leave the growth untri'ed*
> *Of that wide gap.*

He assembles the heroes at a feast. The after-dinner talk is restricted to deeds of war.

> *For of what else could great Achilles tell,*
> *Or others tell with great Achilles there?* [19]

Nestor finally has the floor and while Nestor talks, centuries can slip by. When he has finished, the war is done. So in the journey of Aeneas, a brief expanse of paper holds a copious flow of time. It is a different voyage ·from that of Virgil's hero and might have differed still more; Ovid, poet of the tender loves, shows remarkable restraint in omitting the various replicas of the hero's amour with Dido which, as we learn from the commentary of Servius, legend contained. But this is not the time for a travesty of Aeneas; the tone of the poem is sobering as it approaches the end.

The voyage gets its proper length from the incidental stories, interspersed with diverting effect. While we are listening with Galatea to her monstrous shepherd's serenade, Aeneas is gliding on to his destination. In the last book, the poet leaps down the centuries too precipitously, some critics think, as though he were anxious to wind up his long legend and did not quite know how. If, however, we perceive the ideal issues underneath the narrative, the journey has not been too swift. The poet, with the meaning of Virgil's epic in mind, sees in Roman history a composite harmony of the native sweetness and strength of Italy and the enlight-

enment brought to Italy from without. In the
fourteenth book, the charm of primitive antiquity is set forth in the stories of Picus and
Pomona. In the last book, we have a vision of
a greater Italy, a new Rome, growing by what
it shall absorb from abroad. First comes the
discourse of Pythagoras in which he reveals to
King Numa his doctrine of metempsychosis
and the ultimate truths of life. Here is a bright
cloud of Greek learning, Greek thought, cast
artfully by the poet about the origins of his
country. In a setting of wide historical perspective, with glances back to the cities of
yester-year as well as forward to the majesty
of Rome to come, Ovid inserts a bit of panegyric as impressively sincere as anything in
Virgil:

Famed once was Sparta; once Mycenae throve
And towers of Cecrops and Amphion's towers.
Now dust is Sparta, high Mycenae fell.
Oedipus' Thebes to legend has decayed,
The Athens of Pandion is a name.
Now rise, fame tells, the walls of Dardan Rome;
Where Tiber flows from lordly Apennine,
She lays the great foundations of the world.[20]

Now follows the story of Egeria and that of
Hippolytus, a bit of tragedy not unworthy of

master Euripides. Next is the legend of Cipus, an example of that ancient *virtus*, self-sacrifice for the state, which is the back-bone of Roman character and owes nothing to foreign importation. The next episode marks the appearance of Greece, as Rome unites with her own religion the worship of Aesculapius. The previous stories symbolize remote antiquity; this one brings us to the third century, the time, in Horace's profound epigram,

When captive Greece took its rude victor captive.

This is a turning-point in the history of Rome. The next and last for our poet to record is the Augustan age, with its culminating metamorphosis, the exaltation of Julius Caesar to godhead. History, like geography, is plastic in Ovid's hands. Every island is a floating Delos to him, and centuries may be compressed into decades if he will.

The ending of the last book is thus a monument to Rome. The beginning of that book is a monument of the poet's temperament. His is a philosophy of metempsychosis in a world of flux and flow. Ovid is speaking with gravity again, as at the commencement of the poem. His burlesques of the gods are passing pleasantries and no more reveal his judgment of the deeper verities of life than the pictures of Olympus in the *Aeneid* show us the religion of Virgil. If this is all of Ovid, his poem is indeed, as Sellar would have it, the most irreligious in history. But in the *Aeneid* no less than in the *Metamorphoses*, Olympus can be a stage for comedy; Virgil's tragedies are for humankind. The twilight of the gods was settling before Ovid's time. As early as Aeschylus, reverent spirits brooded over the conflict of primitive and immoral myths with new and higher conceptions of the divine. And apart from that, burlesque can run side by side with worship, except in some cold and colorless creed. Both moods are found in Plautus's *Amphitryo*, which at the beginning presents a most Ovidian Jove, and ends in a lowly adoration of the Divine Benefactor. Both moods are found in Homer. Puritans will find much to shock them in Mediaeval parodies of sacred things, and yet the Middle Ages were the ages of faith. Both Virgil and Ovid bow to something sacred behind the myth. Both reverence the simple piety of simple folk; the beautiful legend of Philemon and Baucis, who entertained deities unawares, is told to silence a scoffer.

It were rash to define Ovid's theology. A vague monotheism may underlie his story of creation. He trusts in the gentleness of heaven, — *mite deum numen*. At the same time, there is more than one Euripidean protest against the injustice of the gods; what is revelry for them is bitter fate for human beings. Still, these are the gods of myth; the poet tacitly appeals to a principle of justice above them.

> *Parer ingiusta la nostra giustizia*
> *Negl' occhi dei mortali ed argomento*
> *Di fede e non d'eretica nequizia.*

Ovid's mind is too subtle, too nomadic, to attach itself to a science. He is too keenly alive to human realities to profess an ultimate scepticism. In the world of magic in which he freely moves, it were hazardous to say what miracles may not come to pass. He can have a fling at scepticism. Orpheus, on entering the world of shades, remarks to Proserpine that he supposes Love is omnipotent there as elsewhere:

> *If Pluto's theft of thee is not a myth.*

This is the *ne plus ultra* of incredulity, the uncertainty of one mythicality about the genuineness of another. I call this a fling at scepticism,— perhaps it is something else.

Ovid is likewise no cynic. For that, he has too lively a sympathy with humble things, with impossible things, like Centaurs. His imagination loves to make the most of a small domain, *Parva sed apta.* He has the skill of a French house-wife *faire des petites économies.* He would applaud Herrick's maxim:

A *little saint best fits a little shrine,*
A *little prop best fits a little vine,*
As *my small cruse best fits my little wine.*[21]

After all our attempts at analysis, Ovid's spirit eludes us. If we call him this or that, he quickly performs a metamorphosis and shows another face. He loves shadings, the slanting intermediates, in Meredith's phrase, the twilights of nature and of the mind, — *tenues parvi discriminis umbrae.* But in the midst of the flowing circumstance of time and space, his spirit, like Shakespeare's, dwells master of itself and creator of whatever world he will. He has written himself into his poem, which not only tells of changing forms but is metamorphosis itself, riding on like a supple river-god, a Proteus of a stream, with a clearness, as Landor says, that shows the depths, passing through different lights and shades and rippling with a different music at every turn, forever changing and forever the same.

The work had not received its author's finishing touches; it was "still growing and still rude," he declares, when Augustus banished him from Rome. He burned his manuscript. Perhaps he might have excised a few touches of false rhetoric and false pathology here and there, — false from audacity and not from lack of taste — but what else could he have done? The poet knows that he has succeeded. At the close he can well declare his immortality, — if, as he adds,

If prophesies of bards have aught of truth.

Previously he had intimated that the devotion of bards to truth is not intense. We are coming out from Ovid's world of shifting dreams by the Ivory Gate.

3. The Poet of the Pagan Year

When with the Virgin morning thou do'st rise,
Crossing thy selfe; come thus to sacrifice . . .
Next to the Altar humbly kneele, and thence,
Give up thy soule in clouds of frankincense.

HERRICK

Protinus accessi ritus ne nescius essem. OVID

AFTER his magical handling of chronology in the *Metamorphoses,* Ovid may have felt something of the pride of the connoisseur in composing a poetical calendar of Roman feasts, a " Pagan Year." To devote a whole poem to religion is a sign of the poet's deepening interests, or rather of the deeper side of his nature flowing more naturally into his verse; the fascination of cults and ceremonies is no new thing to him, as we saw in his earliest love-poetry. His plan in the new poem is to follow the calendar, giving a book to each month and describing the feasts in their turn. Nothing could be more unlike the Protean display of variety in the *Metamorphoses* than this simple design. Ovid's imagination has not failed; he is treating liturgy decently and in order; there will be variety enough of its kind. For the metre, Ovid returns to the elegiac couplet. Propertius had anticipated him in poems on religious rites, which, by the example of Callimachus, the Greek master of them both, are appropriate for elegy. But it is sober elegy. Ovid is no longer the tender singer of the playful loves, but " the busy poet of the days."

Roman religion, one might infer from certain summary treatments of it, is a bare and lifeless round of ceremonies, which neither cheered nor sanctified the life of the worshipper, but were maintained superstitiously as an instrument for binding the gods to their part of the bargain. Give and take; pay the vow, sacrifice the victim, and no plague shall visit the sheep-fold or mildew spoil the standing crops. Fear made the first gods; kings and priests, in the interests of the state, imposed divine worship on their credulous subjects. There is an element of truth in such assertions, which ancient as well as modern authors have made, but the sum of them presents an idea of religion that hardly could have lasted a twelvemonth. We may turn to Walter Pater's *Marius the Epicurean,* where the imaginary picture of the ancient rites of Rome is nearer the living reality than are some authorities on *Römischer Kultus.* To penetrate to the heart of Roman worship in the times of Augustus, we should go to the poets, to Virgil for religious aspiration, to Horace for the worship of the state, to Ovid for the beauty of ritual.

There are several strands in the texture of Roman religion as the contemporaries of Ovid knew it. The rites of earliest Italy had been enlarged with Greek legends and practices, and though philosophy was originally distinct from religion, the latter derived new colorings, particularly from the Platonic and Stoic systems of thought. The veneration of the heroes of old also crystallized into ceremony; St. Romulus has his day in Ovid's calendar. If the primitive Romans are less imaginative than the Greeks, the reason is partly that they were too reverential to treat their gods jocosely. The worship of the *di indigetes* was not necessarily bare because these deities had no domestic history. Tacitus thought the religion of the Hebrews bare because no image was found within the inner temple. The art of Giotto may seem bare to those who are unmoved by his mystic awe. The fancy of the Romans, leaving the gods alone, played freely about the heroes; this was the kind of myth wherewith, as Livy puts it, they hallowed the origins of Rome. The more we must detract from the authenticity of early Roman history, the more we must add to the poetical creativeness of the Romans.

Ovid is deeply interested, perhaps particularly interested, in the faith of his primitive ancestors, in the days when

The stars in annual path free roamed the sky
All unobserved; and yet the gods were nigh.[22]

It was the Golden Age of liberty for the planets, before they were shackled to scientific theory. The gods were worshipped in plain images of straw, but, says the poet, no less reverent was the worship of that straw than of the Roman eagles which symbolized the might of Augustus's divinity. In those happy times, the gods moved freely among men, visiting the cottage unawares. The hearth of Vesta was a sacred thing; the farmer and his family would sit on long benches before the fire and believe that the gods had their place at the table. The shepherd knows that every grove is full of deities. He prays to his goddess Pales for pardon if ever he has entered a forbidden grove, or by peeping about has made the nymphs scamper with the half-goat god at their heels, or if he has lopped off a bough from a sacred tree as browze for a sick sheep, or if in a sudden hail-storm he has driven his little flock into a rustic shrine. These were desperate cases, but the sin had been done. May the goddess have mercy, and grant that he may ne'er look on a Dryad, or Dian at her bath, or rout old Faunus from his noon-day nap!

All Roman poets are liturgical, even Lucretius, who describes the rites of Cybele with no

little zest.[23] Many a solemn measure in Virgil
and Horace sounds most deeply to those who
can hear the same music in the Catholic Mass.
Ovid, too, is fond of liturgical lines, which call
to one another like choristers chanting antiph-
onally. After the flood, says the poet in the
Metamorphoses, Jupiter saw that of the thou-
sands of mankind only two remained. This
statement is not made simply but sung liturgi-
cally, with a bit of rhyme, in a verse and its
response:

Et superesse virum de tot modo milibus unum,
Et superesse videt de tot modo milibus unam.[24]

There are similar passages in the *Fasti*. The
Great Mother of the gods is brought to Rome
in a vessel of state at night-fall. They tie the
cable to a stump of oak and after a slight re-
past, lie down to sleep. At day-break they construct a hearth, offer incense upon it, and cast
off. The liturgical character of the act is not
stated in words but sung in the verse:

Nox aderat: querno religant a stipite funem
Dantque levi somno corpora functa cibo.
Lux aderat: querno solvunt a stipite funem,
Ante tamen posito tura dedere foco.[25]

[81]

Ovid has not merely a liturgical manner at his command. He has an expert's acquaintance with hosts of rites, usual and unusual, and can set them into poetry with vivid charm and delicate sympathy. He describes with zest the merrymakings attending the feast of Anna Perenna, when the people build booths of boughs by the Tiber and drink as many cups as the years they wish to live, — the poet declares that he has seen those who by grace of much potation rivalled the longevity of Nestor or the Sibyl. As they reel home at the end of the day, the crowd cheers them and calls them blessed. A quieter scene is the feast of Terminus, god of the farmer's bounds, a humble god, but ancient, and firm to maintain the true line of division even though the farmer beat him over the head with a ploughshare or a rake. More solemn is the *Parentalia*, the festival of the dead, whose shades are satisfied with the humble offerings of the devout, — garlands and fruit, a pinch of salt thrown on the flames, or loose violets in some potsherd, found in the country road. Pictures like these indicate no dull round of obligations, but the pleasant feasts of immanent deities, to whom costly victims were a less ample oblation than the

[82]

prayers of the poor. Ovid's poem reflects the
colors, gay and sombre, of the life of a people
more deeply penetrated with religion than
people are today.

If Ovid's calendar consisted merely of a
series of festivals and rites described as he describes them, there would be for us life and
variety enough, but not for him. He has not
forgotten his earliest title to fame. Venus, it
would seem, imagines that he has. At the beginning of her own month, April, he makes the
goddess a courteous apology, which would
seem a bit superfluous; for love runs in and
out of the poem as it does in the *Metamorphoses*. There is a Rabelaisian tale of the ass of
Silenus who by an untimely braying inter-
rupted Priapus's wooing of the nymph. The ass
is promptly sacrificed, and has ever since been
sacrificed, to Silenus; what would seem to us
a commendable moral protest was imputed to
the poor beast as original sin. But the gods
are sometimes not nice in ethical distinctions.
Flora, the charming but disreputable goddess
who contests with Jupiter the right to name the
first of May, declares:

> We *gods love honor, altars, festal song;*
> *Like politicians, we're a greedy throng.*

The sinner often moves celestial hate,
Yet oft a victim doth our anger sate.
Jove have I seen, his bolts about to rain,
At whiff of incense drop his arm again.[26]

Such is the message of the wanton goddess of flowers, who at the end of the conversation departs, if not in the odor of sanctity, at least amid an agreeable fragrance. Primitive Italian awe has melted with her into the insubstantial air. Flora is responsible for a bit of what we might call, in the midst of so much liturgy, "blasphemous relief" or, better, the irrepressible bubbling up of the poet's wit.

There is more of this witty irreverence in the poem, and it can intermingle with devotion. Ovid's mind is at its Protean play again. He opens the last of the six books in a serious strain:

A god within us animates the soul
With sacred sparks of the celestial whole.

This mood does not last long. So, then, the poet continues, it is no sin to meet goddesses face to face, as he did! Juno, addressing him respectfully as "founder of the Roman year," asserts her right to name the month of June. Juventa, the bride of Hercules, interrupts her argument boisterously, when Concordia appears, not to reconcile the disputants but to claim the honor for herself. The poet, remembering the unhappiness that Paris brought into the world, refuses to become famous for a *iudicium Nasonis*. He sends the goddesses away without a decision:

> *Paris by arbitration Troy o'erthrew;*
> *Less joy had he from one than woes from two.*

The poet's conversation with Janus is more profitable. Ovid approaches, with the assurance of a modern reporter, salutes the god, as an ancient Italian deity, to whom Greece has nothing similar, and asks why he alone of immortals can see his own back. The god affably consents to be interviewed, and the poet whisks out his note-book. Janus explains that as a veritable antiquity, — *nam sum res prisca* — he goes back to the days of Chaos, at which time he was a shapeless mass. Some of the first experiments at creation, as the reader may verify from Lucretius, were curious; the god is one of those early monstrosities or freaks of nature; that is why he has a face before and behind. However, this peculiarity is put to use. He survives as the fittest creature to become concierge of the sky. After a fusilade of questions, the poet is anxious to know the symbolism of the coin which the devout offer to the god. The latter, smiling with a far-away look of worldly wisdom, points out that long ago customs were simple.

In his small shrine, Jove scarce upright could stand,
And sped clay thunder-bolts with mightiest hand.
With leaves, not gems, adorned Rome's temple
*   stood.*
Himself the statesman gave his sheep their food.
No shame it was to rest the tired head
On a straw pillow in a stubble bed.[27]

But times have changed, — and Janus has changed with them. It is the new Age of Gold, when gods find a better omen in golden coin than in the ancient copper. Despite his antiquity, this god is up-to-date.

We praise old times but use the present age.

In this burlesque, there is a deeper feeling in the lines on antique simplicity, and in those in which Janus dwells on the happy days

When gods could walk the earth
And hospitably sit by human hearth.

The *Fasti,* no less than the *Metamorphoses,* is colored with both Roman and Italian sentiment. There are unforgettable glimpses of the Italy that Virgil glorified in the *Georgics* and the modern traveller loves. Silvia the Vestal, carrying an earthen jar on her head, like a peasant-woman today, goes to the Tiber to fetch water for the sacrifice. Wearied, she sits down on the bank, opens her breast to the cooling breeze and sets in order her dishevelled locks. A glimpse of ancient Italy that may seem only too realistic to some travellers in the modern land is given in the prayer of the business man, addressed to Mercury, god of business men and of thieves.

" *Forgive my perjuries; they're in the past.*
Forgive false prices, for they did not last.
If e'er I sent thee, as I'm sending now,
An affidavit, and then broke my vow;
If e'er I aimed an oath at great Jove's ear,
On the condition that he should not hear;
If god or goddess I have taken in;
Let the wild winds evaporate my sin!
Aye, let my perfidies be clear as day,
If heaven will discount the next thing I say.
Grant me the joy of getting millions quick,
And grant the skill my customers to trick."

[87]

When *thus our merchant-prince puts up his*
prayer,
Old *Hermes chortles in the upper air,*
And *feasts his fancy with the memory fine*
Of *how he cleaned Apollo of his kine.*[28]

Panegyric of Augustus is hard to make convincing when Augustus and Jupiter are almost
convertible terms and when the poet of the
Metamorphoses would magnify Augustus. We
must distinguish between the amorous Jupiter
of Greek myth and the majestic Jupiter of the
Roman Capitol. But that is not easy. Ovid
does his best as though he had not already done
his worst. Augustus would take no offence, —
provided that he had not read the *Metamorpho-*
ses. The verses on March sixth, when Julius
Caesar became Pontifex Maximus, ring true in
the prayer to those ancient gods of Troy that
the hero Aeneas brought on his long journey to
Rome. The *Fasti,* like the *Metamorphoses,* is
a mirror of the poet's mind, with its perpetual
interchanging of grave and gay. It is not prop-
aganda written for Augustus's plans for the
revival of religion, yet beneath the merriment
there is homage to simple piety and a love of
the old-fashioned rite. Though the busy poet
of the days completed but half of his work, it

is the finest monument preserved to us of the liturgy of ancient Rome.

4. THE POET IN EXILE

IN THE year 8 A.D. Ovid's career, hitherto blameless, as he says, was blasted by a thunderbolt from the real and Roman Jupiter. Augustus banished the poet to Tomis on the shores of the Black Sea. A mystery underlies this sentence that possibly may never be solved. Ovid assigns two sorts of offence that had brought the punishment upon him, his poem and his error, — *carmen et error*. The poem is the *Art of Love*, published about eight years before. If that was cause for banishment, it is a wonder that the poet was not banished forthwith, or at least soon after, when in 2 A.D. the performances of the smart set at court culminated in the disgrace of the Emperor's daughter Julia. Ovid's wit, though doing little harm to temperaments like his own, had profaned the mysteries and stimulated intrigue; the *Art of Love* was more, not less, dangerous, than the *Amores* from its very profession that it was perfectly safe. Now in 8 A.D., when the younger Julia, following her mother's example, capped a climax of high living by an amour with Silanus,

Augustus may well have felt that his reform of morals, glorified in the panegyrics of Virgil and Horace, had come to a grievous end. He would have read with a bitter sense of irony Horace's rejoicings at the advent of a time when

Mothers are praised for offspring of like kind.[29]

The Emperor doubtless knew Ovid by reputation; he picked up a copy of the *Art of Love,* — one of those best sellers that potentates do not have time to read — scanned enough of its contents to corroborate his opinion, and acted. He visited light penalties on the guilty pair; Julia lived for the rest of her days in one of the towns of Italy, while Silanus, though he went into voluntary exile, was merely excluded from court. On Ovid, supposedly the high priest of this disastrous cult, was visited the full sum of the Emperor's wrath.

So much for the *carmen.* It was the ostensible cause, and perhaps in itself might have occasioned the poet's disgrace. But there was some deeper offence, something that had touched Augustus to the quick. On Ovid's part, this was merely an " error," a " fault," without a tinge of crime. His eyes, he tells us, were chiefly to blame; like Actaeon, or the peeping

[90]

On dit que l'amour même fut cause en partie . . .
Et qu'il vint tout exprès au fond de la Scythie.

LINGENDES

shepherd in the *Fasti,* he had seen more than he should have seen. What this unhallowed sight was, he does not once suggest. Everybody may have known all about it, but a gentlemanly decency sealed his lips. The guesses of scholars have been various. Some have thought that the plottings of the Empress Livia against the household of her step-children, the Julias included, may have been ultimately responsible for the poet's fate, — a fine bit of tragic irony for the poet of the loves, to perish in a *bataille de dames!* He may have been caught at a gathering of conspirators, or a *séance* of magicians who were scheming by their arts the death of Augustus. Or perhaps he had observed His Majesty himself in some delicate predicament! Perhaps he hit him off in a burlesque. If the gods of Greece and the heroes of Rome, if Jove himself, if Apollo, the favored deity of the Augustan age, can be exhibited on the poet's comic stage, why not the champion of Apollo and counterpart of Jove? There is no evidence that Ovid was specially adverse to the cult of Apollo, which symbolized Augustus's cherished ideals. Ovid is no sectarian; he is not " anti " anything. He could hardly have directed the Emperor's particular attention to the *Meta-*

morphoses if that poem had included a tract against the worship of Apollo. But could Augustus have read the *Metamorphoses* through, he might have thought that performance still more fatal than the *Art of Love* to his programme of religious reform. The tender poet of Jupiter's amours might have been banished even for the *Metamorphoses* alone. But all this is guess-work. We may let the curtain fall once more on the mystery, finding the ultimate cause of the poet's ruin in the words of his confession

"ingenio perii."

Tristia

Car sachiés que toutes vos choses
Sunt en vous-méismes encloses.

JEAN DE MEUN

Ingenio tamen ipse meo comitorque fruorque
Caesar in hoc potuit iuris habere nihil.

OVID

For a nature like Ovid's, banishment to the chill shores of the Euxine Pontus amounted to solitary imprisonment for life. The strictest sort of exile had not been decreed in his case; he retained his property, and eventual return to Rome was not excluded. He immediately bent

his energies to lamenting his fate and securing
his return. The first of his letters from exile
were collected under the appropriate title
Tristia. His favorite metre was also still appropriate; for elegy, by one theory, was originally a mournful form of verse, *flebile carmen*,
and the grief of the lover or the mourning for
a poet of love had traditionally accompanied
love-poems of an entirely different caste. But
Ovid is pouring new wine into the ancient
bottle; it is doubtless his extension of the use
of the elegiac metre in the *Tristia* that
prompted Mediaeval Latin poets to employ it
for any subject whatsoever and led in our own
poetry to the restriction of elegy to mournful
verse.

Ovid's new essay in poetry may seem to reveal a spirit unmanned. Boethius in his dun-
geon wrote no *Tristia*, but a consolation of
philosophy, in which he sought to justify the
ways of God to men. Nothing could banish
Dante from himself. " Shall I not," he declares, " in any place look on the mirror of the
sun and the stars? Can I not under whatever
sky contemplate the sweet and eternal verities? " [30] To Ovid, sun and stars appeared exiled too, if they did not shine on him from the

sky of Italy. No chance for poetry when his world has been tipped upside down:

Songs cannot flow but from a mind serene.[31]

Despite these words of his, Ovid began to write again the moment he got on shipboard and had a new volume well-nigh ready when he reached port. It is an agreeable little book, with touches of pathos, of affection towards his friends, of devotion to his wife. We may positively say, what we had suspected before, that for all his witty audacities, Ovid had a high conception of womanhood and was himself no libertine. He turns to song for consolation. With his castle of delight suddenly demolished, he rebuilds; he adjusts himself, with no little fancy, to a new mythology; his faithful wife is added to the heroines, — a new Penelope. He is Ulysses, tossed about in a somewhat literary storm with the spray moistening his tablets as he writes. Or he is Aeneas, leaving his Troy, not for the city's doom but for his own. There is genuine grief and repentance beneath the badinage; the poem on his departure is his real apology for the *Art of Love*. On his arrival, Ovid composed an encomium of the good ship that had brought him safe to land, and wrote

an introductory address to his little book as it
fared forth on its hazardous voyage across the
seas and its still more hazardous wanderings
about Rome. He bids it steer clear of the
Palatine and make for the poet's house, where
it will find its brother-volumes, most of them
displaying their titles unabashed, though

> *Three in a corner dark their heads hang low,*
> *For teaching love, which no one does not know.*

Then there are those fifteen volumes of metamorphoses, lately rescued from the extinction
that had befallen their author.

> *Amongst their transformations, pray relate*
> *A postscript legend on my shattered state.*

Ovid's first volume, we see, is not unduly lu-
gubrious. We wonder if he is taking his exile
seriously enough. Perhaps he thought that the
time was not far distant when he could return
to his pleasant garden, and settle himself com-
fortably again, with pen and tablet, on his
accustomed couch.

The next effort of the exile was to transmit to
the Emperor, probably in 9 A.D., an elaborate
apology; it forms Book II of the *Tristia*. He
divides his offence into his *carmen* and his *er-*

ror, says no word on the latter, unwilling to
open his wounds again, and presents a lengthy
defence of the poem, to show that he ill deserves the title of " teacher of obscene adul-
tery." Had he not warned all matrons away, at
the beginning of the work? He was only having
a little fun.

> *My life is pure, though sullied is my page;*
> *My merry Muse frequents the comic stage.*
> *Most of my verse is sheer mendacity;*
> *She gives herself more license than to me.*

This is a familiar apology, presented by Martial, Ausonius, Herrick and others. In reality,
the libertine whose life is sullied but whose
page is pure, is, like Chaucer's pardoner, much
more beneficial for the morals of posterity.

> *For, though myself be aful vicious man,*
> *A moral tale yet I yow telle can.*

Ovid next points out that he is not the only
poet who has written on the forbidden theme.
The examples that he cites make up a veritable
manual of Greek and Latin poetry. He himself
had been guilty before, if guilt that was. True
enough, the *Amores* is ostensibly a more fla-
grant transgression than the veiled rascality of

the *Art of Love*. But what did he hope to gain
by such argument? Ten volumes of exculpa-
tion of his *carmen* could have made his case
no better. He proves too much, especially, with
ill-timed wit, in dragging in the saintly Virgil
among the salacious.

The happy bard who thine Aeneid *did sing,*
Arms and the man to Dido's couch could bring.
In all that work no tale's more often read
Than of those mates in lawless passion wed.

Instead of acknowledging his sin, the culprit
would demonstrate that he is no worse than
Virgil! He may mean to cry " Mea culpa, mea
maxima culpa," but he jests in the confessional.
One line gives evidence of a contrite heart. He
declares that he is sorry for his wit and for his
false judgment:

Paenitet ingenii iudiciique mei.

Had he sent just this verse to Augustus it
might have had some effect. Alas, instead of
repenting of his wit, he continues to exhibit it
throughout his apology. The thing is too pro-
vokingly clever. Worst of all, he proceeds to
reprove the Emperor himself for lending his
sanction to other indecencies, such as the rough

Roman vaudeville, and then being suddenly shocked at the *Art of Love*. Ah, why, the poet exclaims, had he not had the sense to write for the vulgar stage, where gentlemanly adulterers are heroes and the canny wife dupes her stupid husband. And, most unkindest cut of all, the writer of mimes draws a huge salary, while Ovid draws exile! Just reflect, your Majesty, on the kind of performances that you have witnessed in your own exhibitions!

Such hast thou seen, and given us to see,
So kind a sovereignty resides in thee.
Thou, on whom looks the world, with thine own
* eyes*
Lenient hast gazed on stage adulteries.

In fine, unless the Emperor's intelligence was encased in a hide of elephantine thickness, the poet could have hardly expected a reprieve for an appeal like this. Whatever Ovid's intention was, this *apologia pro vitiis suis* is addressed not to Augustus but to posterity.

The remaining books of the *Tristia* bring us down into the year 12 A.D. They show an increase of seriousness in Ovid, as he comes more and more to realize that his missives are producing no result. His thoughts turn to death.

He hopes that his ashes may be decently interred in Rome. Again his spirit rises, and refuses to be overborne by its afflictions. He turns to the Muse, who is his rest and healing, his guide and companion. She can transport him from the Danube's bank to the slopes of Helicon, or, better still, to his beloved Rome, where he can talk as of old with his friends the livelong day:

They're here, although beyond the body's call;
With the mind's vision, I can see them all.[32]

After all, Ovid can free himself from his iron bars with something of the defiance of a Lovelace or a Boethius. His power to create a new mythology is still active. He promises his loyal wife an immortality in song, with Alcestis and Andromache, — and, let us not forget, with Corinna. One of the letters is to the maiden Perilla, probably the poet's step-daughter; she is sitting by her mother's side, busy, he hopes, with those studies that once he had shared with her. He contrasts his own surroundings, the horrors of the winter, when the natives wear coats of fur, icicles hang on the beard and wine is served in frozen chunks. Yet violets come in the spring and boys and girls pick them merrily. The poet finds himself a somewhat useless member of the society of Tomis, where everybody speaks Gothic, a few Greek, and nobody Latin. Among these aborigines, Ovid is in the plight of Horace's sane man among the insane.

I'm barbarous here, whom none can understand.[33]

Still, he manages to learn both Getic and Sarmatic and suggests a new and wintry theme for a pastoral, with a shepherd piping a frozen lay through his helmet.

As one ends the five volumes of *Tristia*, it is patent that bit by bit, a feeling of dreariness or even despair is closing in about the poet. He recounts his bodily ailments with the preciseness of a chronic invalid, — malaria, insomnia, emaciation, indigestion, jaundice. His spirit is breaking. Several times he feels that his end is approaching, and writes what he may well have thought the last of his poems. One of these contains his epitaph:

I that lie here, the bard of playful love,
The poet Ovid, perished for my play.
Oh passing lover, scorn not thou to pray
That no ill chance my restful bones may move.[34]

Last Works

No change, no pause, no hope! Yet I endure.

SHELLEY

Fortiter Euxinis immoriemur aquis

OVID

Ovid's exiled Muse was fertile in other themes than *Tristia*. He composed, in the manner of Callimachus, a poem of curses, entitled *Ibis,* and directed against an ancient enemy. Six hundred and forty-four verses of malediction in one breath! Still, there is little vehemence behind them; it might seem that this enemy, like Corinna, was imaginary and composite, — an objectification of the poet's many protests against his fate. What astounds the reader, and often baffles the scholar, is Ovid's profound acquaintance with rare myths. Either he is lying, or, if he really had no books in Tomis, his powers of memory deserve to be recorded among the prodigies of antiquity. This is a fable for those critics who assume some handbook of mythology or, if they are liberal, two handbooks, as the main source of the *Metamorphoses,* not observing that the poet himself was a walking library of myths.

Ovid's learning is no less apparent in a poem on the art of fishing, *Halieutica,* of which only a fragment remains. The work aroused the admiration of no less a scientist than the elder Pliny, who found fish in Ovid's list not mentioned elsewhere, and concluded that the poet must have noted them in the Euxine Pontus.[35] Ovid speaks as an angler of some experience. One of his couplets was chosen, not many years ago, as a motto by an excellent authority on sea-fishing:[36]

There's much in chance; trawl your line anywhere.
When you would least expect, a fish is there.

These verses, to be sure, are from another work of the poet's, — intended for fishers of men — but the principle applies also to sea-fishing.

The stars were visible from Tomis, and Ovid wrote a poem, which has not come down to us, on astronomy, entitled, after the famous work of the Greek poet Aratus, *Phaenomena*. He had been preceded in this subject, among the Romans, by Cicero and by his own contemporary Germanicus Caesar. In honor of the latter, he wrote a dedication of the *Fasti* and gave that work a partial revision. Here and there we can detect an added verse as in the lines on his birth-place, pathetically contrasted with his present home among the Goths. There is a

brave utterance in contempt of exile, which if
not inserted at the time of the revision, is
grimly prophetic of his coming fate.

As birds the air and fish the ocean roam,
So a bold heart finds all the world a home.[37]

We have evidence of other works composed
by Ovid in exile, an epithalamium for his friend
Fabius Maximus, an ode of jubilation on the
triumph of Tiberius in 13 A.D., a threnody on
the death of Augustus, and even a panegyric
in the Getic tongue on the imperial family. A
poem on the nut-tree, *Liber Nucis,* though long
regarded as of doubtful genuineness, is in all
probability an allegory of his exile; the tree
complains that innocent as it is, every passer-
by pelts it with stones. Not its own fault but
its very productivity is the cause of its ill
treatment; the tree wonders that the Emperor,
who protects all, can suffer it to be thus perse-
cuted.

Love, the poet declares, is an impossible
theme for him. Still, Cupid appears to him in
a vision and is asked to intercede for him;
everybody else had been asked, and, besides,
Cupid is the cousin of Augustus. Cupid swears
by his torch and his arrows, by his mother and

by Caesar's head that the *Art of Love* is perfectly proper and never was meant for matrons. Here is the old Ovid, in command of a genial and saucy wit, particularly in that oath by Caesar's head. Could he have continued that vein for such works as the *Double Heroides*, which by certain metrical tests best fit in with the poetry of his exile? It seems unlikely. Ovid's sprightliness still comes in flashes, — flashes against a prevailing background of gloom.

Epistulae Ex Ponto

The letters of the latter part of Ovid's exile show nothing new in the poet's genius or his mood, except that whatever hope he had entertained of a restoration has gone for good; the twilight of the *Tristia* is settling into night. At least he can now name the friends to whom he writes; it is no longer dangerous for them to be known as his correspondents. The number of them is amazing; there seems to have been nobody worth knowing, at least in the literary set, that Ovid did not know. His appeals do not cease, fruitless though they must be. They become monotonous, and he tells us so. Yet they become so varied that he can construct a new art, — safer, and less effective than his former invention — an *ars precandi!* His pupil is no longer Corinna, but that other heroine of mythology, Penelope; she is urged to apply the new precepts in a final address to Livia.

Ovid dwells several times on the sacred bond that unites fellow-poets; he goes back in fond reminiscence to his travels with Macer, in Asia, in Sicily, at the fountain in Syracuse where Arethusa had made her way up from the deep!

> *Something it is together seas to brave,*
> *Together pay our vows to gods that save.*[38]

Again, the poet's fancy takes him back to the little garden which he used to water with his own hands, and in which he had set out some plants — are they still alive? He thinks of taking up farming in his new abode; he must learn the calls that Gothic oxen know, — he will make them mind! This pastoral description recalls the delightful account in the *Metamorphoses* of the wooing of Pomona; the altered context gives the repeated words a vivid pathos. In fact, reminiscence now brings him pain; the dwelling of his mind on Rome freshens the grief of exile. The poet anticipates

Francesca's bitter epigram that it is sorrow's crown of sorrow to remember happiness in misery.[39]

There are reflections on immortality in the letters from the Pontus, but the poet is less interested in his own immortality than in that which his power of song can confer on others, — on the Emperor, on Cotta, and above all, on his wife. Yes, the gods themselves, if it be not blasphemy to say it, he declares, depend for a part of their majesty on the poet's song. This is indeed a subdued sort of blasphemy for Ovid; there are no divine burlesques in the poems of his exile.

Ovid's studies in Gothic had progressed, and he had made friends among the uncouth inhabitants. Ovid is the least snobbish of men; he craved sympathy and society. "If I have said anything bad about Gothland," he writes a friend, "please assume that I meant the country and not the people, — the people are not a bad lot." Ovid read one of his poems in the vernacular to a native, to the latter's delight. Another told him, as a bit of local tradition, the story of Iphigenia in Tauris. If this incident is as mythical as the tale, it only shows that the Goths have entered with Corinna and

Penelope into the poet's imaginary world of living myths.

But more and more the poet's fancy weakens, or turns into a morbid nervousness. The dream becomes a nightmare; he is fighting on a Gothic battle-field, grazed by the enemy's arrows, shackled with their bonds. He rehearses his ailments again, with an unpleasant wealth of circumstance. His present existence is a life in death. He would welcome a metamorphosis, — not to a conscious being but to a thing of wood or stone. He fights to the end; his is no coward's death. All his strength fails but the mind conquers all. Aye, he will die bravely by the Pontic Sea. But the fight is over; Ovid has his death-blow. The last lines of his book, and for all we know, of his life, are these:

> *All have I lost; enough of life remains*
> *To furnish substance for my spirit's pains.*
> *Stab on. The torture can no further go;*
> *There is no place for yet another blow.*

II. OVID THROUGH THE CENTURIES

Si quid habent veri vatum praesagia, vivam.

OVID

Compagni d'alto ingegno e da trastullo
Di quei che volentier già 'l mondo lesse, —
L'un era Ovidio.

PETRARCH

Among all the poets who take rank merely as story-tellers
and creators of mimic worlds, Ovid still stands supreme.

GILBERT MURRAY

OVID, the poet of changing forms, was aware that his exile was for himself a metamorphosis. If he could have followed the career of his posthumous self, he would have noted, presumably with amusement, many a transformation which ideas about his character, his purposes and his art were to undergo. He found himself famous at an early age; the lays of the mysterious Corinna were sung all over town, and some of his poems, even after his exile, were rendered in the theatres to the accompaniment of song and dance. Exile had threatened the extinction of his works when he burned his copy of the *Metamorphoses* and the libraries ejected his works from their shelves. But all copies of his greatest work had not been destroyed, and the others were doubtless circulated as before. The sensational advertisement given to the *Art of Love* could hardly have interfered with its sale. Ovid was a man's man, — and something of a lady's man as well — and throughout his career had many friends among the poets about town. These friends took care that his works were not forgotten. Some of his verses, in his time or later, were scribbled on the walls of Pompeii. Before his death, busts were made of him and his features were engraved on gems; unfortunately, no certified copy of his likeness remains today.

Eventually, Ovid became a school-book. This fate befell the *Metamorphoses* at the hands of a certain, or uncertain, Lactantius Placidus. Ovid's comedies of the gods and his studies of human moods were relieved of their sparkle and reduced to the lowest terms of fact *in usum puerorum.*

Turn what he would to verse, his toil was vain;
The sober teacher made it prose again.

This is the first of the posthumous metamorphoses of Ovid.

Ovid's fame among writers and critics of literature under the Empire had a somewhat chequered course. Eminent men of letters applauded him, with reservations. If imitation is the best token of praise, he was reckoned among the immortals by the age of Nero and that of Trajan. Seneca, for instance, in his plays, drew abundantly from Ovid's matter and manner. The verdict that he pronounces on our poet's slips into banality falls heavily on his own head. He differs from Ovid in taking his own absurdities seriously.

In following the experiences of the posthumous Ovid, we should expect, besides frequent metamorphoses, a Pythagorean resort of his spirit to other poets' forms. His first reincarnation, with the necessary adaptation to his new environment, is in Martial. Martial is a sort of proletarian Ovid. Like Ovid, he has a sprightly, kaleidoscopic mind, but is several grades beneath him, morally and spiritually. He is a parasite of greater appetite than taste, ready to feed on whatever is cast to him, offal or ambrosia. Ovid is audacious: Martial is unabashed. *Et pudet et dicam,* — "Ashamed I am, and yet I'll say it," declares Ovid; *non pudet et dicam,* expresses Martial. He has Ovid's abandon, which is the ethical corollary of a philosophy of metamorphosis, without that *savoir faire* which prevented Ovid from ever becoming vulgar. Like Ovid, Martial makes no pretences. He has wit and feeling and a dainty grace, — on occasion.

Juvenal seems an utter contrast to Ovid, but Ovid has the makings of a moralist, as the Middle Ages were aware. He does not cry sermons from the house-tops, but his works are stored with acute observations on men and morals which, if the context be forgotten, might be fitted into a letter of St. Paul's or a satire of Juvenal's. Both poets declare that beauty is no aid to chastity. One says:

Lis est cum forma magna pudicitiae,

the other:

Rara est adeo concordia formae
Atque pudicitiae.

Metre aside, which is which? [40] In a stretch of seven lines in which this epigram appears in Juvenal, there are four reminiscences of Ovid. The weeping moralist turns to the laughing for counsel now and then.

[111]

We may follow the literature of the later Empire and note Ovid's presence here and there. He was one of the standard authors. But except in Martial, his influence was not profound. His spirit was still in exile.

1. OVID IN THE MIDDLE AGES

WHEN the Dark Ages swept over Europe, Ovid was submerged, nor did he make much impression on the writers of the Carolingian Renaissance. Ludwig Traube, an immortal name in the history of Mediaeval studies, aptly termed the Carolingian period of literature *aetas Vergiliana*. Virgil was the supreme model for the epic that glorified the ideals of the Emperor in an age of renaissance, and for a new and delightful pastoral that embodied a popular theme in the ancient form. Ovid's day was yet to come. His ghost would say, again, if it crossed from Tomis to Aix la Chapelle:

I'm barbarous here, whom none can understand.

In the latter part of the eleventh century, our poet came at last to his own. If the Middle Ages had been slow in claiming him, they now made up for lost time. Nothing could be more happy than Traube's title of *aetas Ovidiana* for this period, which includes the twelfth century and runs the length of the thirteenth. First of all, Ovid's works were taken into the schools; they were regarded as an essential element in a liberal education. Nor did the Mediaeval master leave the text of Ovid unexplained. The presence of glosses is apparent in manuscripts of various of his works as early as the ninth century, and by the twelfth, a most thorough method of interpretation had been evolved, in which we see that the amatory poems were not always subjected to a mystical interpretation. They were understood in the Middle Ages as they are today. Many choice passages from Ovid were culled for *florilegia,* or "bouquets," the flowers in which were picked to delight the nose, not merely to exercise the hands. All the works of Ovid have their place in a more ample library than a five-foot shelf, the *Biblionomia* of Richard de Fournival, chancellor of the cathedral of Amiens in the thirteenth century. Hugo of Trimberg, in a poem written in 1280 on the authors that no gentleman should neglect, thus pays his respects to Ovid in doggerel verse:

Master Ovid cometh next,
Jolly dog and witty.
Fragrant posies of rich thought
Grow in many a ditty.
If the order you would learn
Of each and every poem,
Follow but the titles through,
And you'll quickly know 'em.

The *Art of Love* is not lacking in this list.

i. ELEGIAC COMEDIES

The Carolingians, though mainly the disciples of Virgil, had taken kindly to Ovid's elegiac distich, and employed it for all sorts of themes. A new and more skilful use of this metre is to be noted in the eleventh century, and is nowhere displayed with greater delicacy than by Hildebert of Lavardin (†1134), who ended his career as Archbishop of Tours. Hildebert, like other poets in the Middle Ages, is master of two kinds of verse, the one simple and generally unmetrical, appropriate for a rustic singer as he pours forth his devotion in a hymn. But the poet is only momentarily rustic; he is writing in a certain style; he has not forgotten his quantities. Hildebert could also compose elegiacs with an easy grace that would

[114]

have excited Ovid's admiration. He is at his
best in a poem elegiac in form, tragic in spirit,
called *Mathematicus*. Its peer in comedy is his
poem on the story of Susanna, *Versus de Sancta
Susanna*.[41] Matter of this kind would ordi-
narily go into a Biblical epic. Hildebert turns
it into a little drama in elegiac verse. The lines
on Susanna at her bath, — the heat of the
summer day, her haste, her hesitant testing of
the water and quick plunge into it, her innocent confidence in her solitude, contrasting with
the leering glances of the old men — show
Ovid's dexterous rapidity, a mastery of his
rhetorical effects, and an apt use of his phrases.

Aestus erat, calor instabat, sol flammeus undas
    Iusserat immemores frigoris esse sui . . .
Illuc invitant Susannam balnea; surgit,
    Huc properat; fraudem nescit inesse loco.
Tentat aquam; laudat tentatam; nuda subintrat
    Laudatam; nudam vidit uterque senum;
Vidit et incaluit.

Such verse might be written in the hey-day of
the Renaissance or by some admirer of Ovid
in the Augustan Age.

Hildebert's poem is the best representative
of a flourishing Mediaeval variety that, start-

ing with the imitation of Plautus and Terence
in elegiac verse, turned more and more to
Ovid for matter as well as manner. In some
of the specimens, the wit is exceedingly coarse.
Woman fares badly in these comedies. She
whose charm has adorned the tale is used to
point the awful moral. Ovid, while largely responsible for the creation of this literary form,
would not approve the crude lack of courtesy
that its coarser examples exhibit. He would
have conveyed the same satire with an art that
even the fair victim would have found delect-
able.

ii. THE TALE

A tradition which Ovid did not found but
which he helped to perpetuate is that of the
novel or tale. Greek romance, and Latin, as
represented by Petronius and Apuleius, handed
over something of its spirit to Christian hagiog-
raphy; the lives of the saints contain many
good stories. Various waifs and strays from
the ancient authors were floating about, and
attracted similar matter that came in from
India or was disseminated by the Arabs. These
were increased by a host of popular *fabliaux*.
Stories in the Latin, accompanied by a proper

moralization, were collected in the *Gesta Romanorum*. At the end of the tradition stand those immortal *raconteurs,* Boccaccio and Chaucer. It is natural that some of Ovid's stories should be taken from their settings and remoulded into popular form. Thus the tale of Pyramus and Thisbe, which Ovid alone had rescued from oblivion, appears in two Latin poems of the thirteenth century, then in Old French, German and Netherlandish. Thisbe is among the good women whose legends Chaucer immortalizes; Gower has the story in his *Confessio Amantis;* the youthful and ardent Boccaccio tells it in *L'Amorosa Fiametta;* the aged and scholastic Boccaccio retells it in his treatise *De Claris Mulieribus.* Tasso is not wearied of repeating it; in Spanish literature we see it in Montemayor; then it is caught up in tragedy, comedy and farce in the drama of all the European countries; Bottom's performance in *A Midsummer Night's Dream* has a noble lineage behind it.

iii. VAGABOND POETRY AND SATIRE

The jolly vagabonds, or Goliards, whose poetry John Addington Symonds illustrated in a little volume of attractive title and not disappointing contents, found much in Master Ovid well suited to their needs. He is the chief priest of their order, with Horace second in the hierarchy. They have learned the arts of love and sing without restraint of the modes and mysteries of Venus, sometimes with a merry Macaronic refrain.

> *Audi bela mia,*
> *Mille modos Veneris*
> *Da hizevaleria.*

In sadder vein, the bard laments the changes of Fortune and expounds the law of her mutability as Ovid had done in the *Tristia,* or he tells of a new sort of metamorphosis in a scathing denunciation of the stingy rich, who, instead of bestowing their garments on the poor poet, have them refitted for themselves in another shape; he himself manages to remould the first verse of Ovid's poem into good Goliardic form.

> *In nova fert animus*
> *Dicere mutata*
> *Vetera, vel potius*
> *Sunt inveterata.*

In another mood, he displays the schoolboy's exultation at a holiday, when he can fling aside

Nasonis carmina, vel aliorum pagina, and fare forth to the green fields. Again, in *Phyllis and Flora,* one of the best of Mediaeval debates, the poet follows the gay cavalcade to the Court of Love, where fawns and nymphs are sporting in the woods, and Silenus, still as disreputable as Ovid pictures him in the *Art of Love,* rides up on his donkey.

> *"Ho!", he shouts in gurgling tonès,*
> S*tepping* pedetentim.
> *Fain he'd join the Maenads' cry;*
> *Wine and age prevent him.*

The case of Knight *versus* Cleric is tried, and with no slight help from Ovid, the verdict is reached that the Cleric is the greater expert in the art of Love. The most tremendous homage paid to our poet is in a graceful *amorosa visione,* modelled on one of the letters *Ex Ponto.* Cupid appears in the watches of the night, and laments that the high standard of Ovid's amorous precepts is maintained no longer: *o tempora, o mores!* Each strophe in this poem is capped with a resonant hexameter from the *Art of Love* or the *Remedies.* The prophet himself is speaking in reproof of a degenerate age!

The verse of the Goliards is found as early
as the ninth century. Collections were made of
the various poems, gay and grave, amatory,
convivial, political, religious, which these wan-
dering minstrels sang at courts and monasteries.
At least as early as the tenth century, somebody hit on the happy idea of creating an
eponymous hero. Whatever their name may
mean, they ultimately claimed descent from
Goliath, who had become in popular fancy a
close rival to Satan, more interesting and lov-
able than Satan, because more human. We
have poems on the confession of Golias, his
sermon, his complaint to the Pope, his address
to the person who stole his purse, and his advice (dissuasive) on matrimony, his elevation
to the Bishopric, his metamorphosis, and his
apocalypse. This lively fiction serves the poet
as a medium for satirizing foibles of the laity
and corruption in the Church; it should not,
however, be taken too seriously as a " picture
of the times." The spirit of Ovid is manifest
in the creation of this master of the sons of
Belial, and there are marked resemblances to
Ovid in the life and poetry of one of the known
Goliardic minstrels of the twelfth century, who

went under the name of the Archipoeta of Cologne.

In the vernacular poetry of France and Germany, the Troubadours and the *Minnesänger,* who continue the tradition of the Goliards, turn back, like them, to Ovid for imagery, themes and part, at least, of his " art " and " remedies " of love. Whatever the poets may have thought of Corinna, a certain generalizing or symbolistic spirit in their poetry suggests the *Amores,* and one of their most delightful inventions comes, it would seem, direct from Ovid. This is the *alba* or *tageliet,* the song at dawn, in which the lover, like Ovid's gallant, upbraids the day for tearing him all too soon from the arms of his lady.

The vein conspicuous in the poems on Goliath flows copiously in Walter Map's *Distinctiones,* a glorious medley, a mirror of life as he saw it at the court of Henry II, and in all the world of man. Among Map's stories some are taken from Ovid, — Myrrha and Leucothea, for example. In recounting his triumphs in a debate with the heretical Waldensians, he exploits their ignorance of theology by remarking that they could have driven a better course of argument, had they not, like Phaëthon, been unaware of the names of the horses. In the thirteenth century, Nigellus Wireker, Map's peer in satire, shows fools their image in his *Speculum Stultorum,* which tells the story of an ass who lost his tail and in compensation endeavored to study theology at Paris. The poem is written in admirably Ovidian elegiacs. It is one of the best satires ever directed against the parade of learning.

Ovid is a master of parody, and parody of all things above, beneath and on the earth was one of the delights of the Middle Ages. Blasphemy has more point, and less sting, in an age of faith, because it is the obverse of devotion. With Mediaeval freedom in mind, we may turn back with a new intelligence to Ovid's blithe comedy of the gods, enjoy its irreverence, and then accompany the author, in a proper spirit of worship, to the celebration of some ancient rite. Ovid has his place, inevitably, in the mock solemnities of the Middle Ages. A grand council is held in spring-time at Remiremont, an assembling of the Court of Love to try the familiar case of Knight *versus* Cleric as adepts in the art of love. No men are admitted to the solemn assize, — only women and priests. A damsel opens the ceremony by reading, as a *quasi evangelium,* selections from the " Precepts of the Illustrious Master Ovid." At the end, a dreadful anathema is pronounced against the Knights, followed by their excommunication.

If Ovid is Evangelist, why not Pope? He is, in a poem of the twelfth century, a satire on a jealous priest, for whose admonition his authority is cited:

> *In just decree Pope Ovid swore,*
> *One woman may have loves galore.*

iv. ROMANCE AND EPIC

Mediaeval imagination delighted to make over heroic characters and episodes into terms of romance, to invite the great figures of antiquity to march down the centuries and make themselves at home in the Middle Ages; the past is plastic in the author's hands. It is the same process that ran a vigorous course in the Hellenistic age of Greek literature and culminated in Ovid himself. He was the first of the Mediaeval romancers. He would have enjoyed seeing his stories of Pyramus, Narcissus, Byblis and Phaëthon extracted from their context and retold in what to the Mediaeval author seemed a modern way. The presence of the ancient poet is also evident in the lengthier romances, those of Crestien de Troyes as well as those which deal with ancient subjects, such as the anonymous *Enéas* and the *Roman de Troie* of Benoît de Sainte-More. The latter poem is a kind of Mediaeval Homer, at several removes; the former is the Mediaeval Virgil. The authors are not illiterate yokels, peering at antique figures through a mist of Mediaeval ignorance. They are cultivated gentlemen who know the Classics well. They are following the rule of an established literary form and adjusting their material to it. In contrast to these romances, and in deliberate contrast, other poets retold ancient stories in the Latin heroic hexameter with a closer conformity to history. Such works deserve the name of epic rather than romance. Thus Joseph of Exeter in the twelfth century wrote a poem *De Bello Troiano* in very decent Latin verse, and applying the same method to a contemporary subject, sought to immortalize the Crusades in his *Antiocheis*. Similarly, the story of Alexander the Great received a twofold treatment. The career of the

Macedonian, something of a romance even in its strictly historical form, had been embellished with marvels from various sources, and it furnished the theme for several romances in the popular tongues. Ovid has contributed something to their making. For instance, the author of the Spanish poem, *Libro de Alexandre,* in the thirteenth century, imitates him in more than one passage. But Ovid's influence is no less obvious in the soberer Latin epic *Alexandreis* which Gualterus de Insulis wrote a hundred years earlier.

V. ARTS OF LOVE AND THE KNIGHTLY CODE

The Renaissance of the twelfth century was, among other things, an age of knight-errantry and courtly love. The poets of chivalry accepted as a standard authority, with some modifications, Ovid's gay text-book on the art of love. Crestien de Troyes translated it, and though the translation is lost, Ovid is abundantly present in the poet's romances. If the historical Ovid took Paris and Helen from Homeric epic and metamorphosed them into figures for his comedy of love, the posthumous Ovid assisted Crestien in a similar abstraction

[125]

of Lancelot and Guinevere from Celtic fairy-legend, and a similar adaptation of their characters to his romance.

In the next century, Ovid's poem is immediately the inspiration of various poetical treatises on the art of love. From France, Ovid passes to Spain, and furnishes many suggestions for the *Libro de Buen Amor* of the Arcipreste de Hita, Juan Ruiz.

The acme of the Mediaeval transformation of Ovid's treatise is reached in the *Romance of the Rose,* one of the greatest works of the period and of all time. It is a composite production by two very different authors. Guillaume de Lorris, probably between 1225 and 1230, began a romance in the form of a vision. A lover in his dream wanders amid a garden of enchantment, where the Rose, the symbol of his loved one, is guarded in a castle. With the help of the god of love, Amors, he is about to pluck the rose, when the poem abruptly ends; the author, after some four thousand lines, had not finished his work. The treatment is leisurely, for Mediaeval romancers were not pressed for time; like other undertakings of the period, their work was done *sub specie aeternitatis.* An air of dreamy mysticism, *la douce savor de la rose,* pervades the story. The poet takes much from Ovid, but what is taken is absorbed and refined. The sentiment of love is as pure, and as passionate, as in some of the later Mediaeval hymns to the Blessed Virgin, the Rose of Heaven.

Forty years later, the work was completed by Jean Clopinel, or Chopinel, de Meun. He enters at the eleventh hour and allows no plucking of the rose for over fifteen thousand verses more. The Lover is not to win without knowing what he wins and why. Jean de Meun is no dreamer, but a scholar, versed in all the Latin Classics, a philosopher, familiar with ancient and contemporary thought, and a satirist, alive to the weaknesses of nobles and churchmen and women. He is likewise a poet and a wit, and doubtless knew full well that he was straining the plot to the limits of its elasticity. The Lover still dreams his dream, and, at the far-off end, plucks the Rose; but the poem has been changed from a romance into what the author calls it, "A Mirror of Love." It is a grand debate among diverse types of thought and feeling. Ovid and Boethius clash at the start, and after other contestants have had their say, Ovid emerges triumphant. He has, in the

process, been considerably reformed. Perhaps
the most profitable of all his metempsychoses
is that in the genius of Jean de Meun.

vi. FORGERIES

A great name attracts to itself both interesting stories, told originally about somebody
else, and seemingly characteristic works, which
somebody else had written. A number of such
writings clusters about Ovid's name. In the
twelfth century, the multitudinous Ovidians of
that period not only wrought out a new elegiac
comedy in Ovid's spirit, but sought fame, at
the expense of their identity, by ascribing some
of their performances to Ovid himself. A
comedy of enormous vogue and influence, entitled *Pamphilus sive de Amore,* was perhaps
not attributed to Ovid at the start. The author
of *The Flea* (*De Pulice*) may have wished to
provide his master with something to match
The Gnat (*De Culice*) ascribed to the youthful
Virgil. Other intruding bits are: *The Fall of
Troy, Money, The She-Wolf, The Louse, Book
of the Three Maidens, The Rustic, The Wonders of the World,* — these titles indicate the
range of topics on which Ovid was made,

whether by accident or intention, to have written. In the case of the forgeries, the perpetrators should not be regarded as literary bandits, laying dark schemes to fool an innocent public; they are rather confederates of the eminent men of letters who startled our generation not many years ago with the publication of a " Fifth Book " of Horace's *Odes*.

The most famous of these Mediaeval hoaxes is the poem called *The Hag (De Vetula)*, known almost surely to be the production of Richard de Fournival in the thirteenth century. The author asserts that the work was found in the times of the Emperor Vastasius (1222–1255) in Ovid's tomb in Colchis! To understand the character of this fiction, we must bear in mind the Mediaeval fondness for romances, and for a particular variety, still inadequately studied, that may well be called historical romance. Its nature may be partly illustrated by the vernacular poems on ancient themes at which we have glanced, and is still more evident in the work called *Dolopathos*, written by Johannes de Alta Silva at the close of the twelfth century. This author, starting with the familiar story of the Seven Sages, deliberately gives it an ancient setting with

Virgil, the magician, as the hero. He is exceedingly well read in the ancients, Ovid included, and is perfectly familiar with Virgil's real character, but he moulds that character to fit his design, just as he shapes the matter of his story to fit the ancient background. Chaucer applies the same art in his *Troilus,* as we have recently learned to see.[42]

In precisely this fashion, the author of the *Vetula* introduces Ovid in an appropriate rôle; he has been transmuted into a hero of romance. The Hag is the ugly old nurse of a maiden with whom the poet is in love. With a stratagem that recalls a scene from the *Fasti,*[43] she promises the lover a rendezvous with her mistress, and at the appointed hour takes her mistress's place. The girl marries another, and Ovid must wait twenty years for the man to die; by that time, his lady is *vetula* herself. Ovid then decides that the best love is the love of learning. The closing book, which somewhat suggests the *Convivio* of Dante, is a series of meditations on philosophy, astrology and religion. Ovid reasons in an orthodox way on various theological problems, sums up the heathen prophecies of the Virgin's Son, and concludes with a prayer to the Virgin. The poem had a wide vogue, and was translated into the vernacular. The *jeu d'esprit* was taken more seriously, perhaps, than even its author had anticipated.

vii. OVID'S TRANSFORMATIONS

We are now to follow our poet in a series of mental and moral transformations which his posthumous spirit, aided by the lively imagination of the Middle Ages, was called on to perform. First, he dons the sober disguise of a moralist.

Ovidius Ethicus

Mediaeval thinkers were quick to see that beneath Ovid's persiflage runs a vein of sobriety and moral acuteness. Juvenal, we noted, could study Ovid to good effect, for Ovid, as Landor remarks, " with all his levity, had more unobtrusively sage verses than any, be he Roman or Athenian." Landor was anticipated by Chaucer. In his *Tale of Meliboeus,* translated from a Latin work of the thirteenth century by Albertano of Brescia, he preaches a fine sermon on true friendship, with illustrations chosen both from Holy Scripture and from the Pagans. The work is a notable monument of Christian humanism. Ovid appears here in good company, with Seneca and St. Paul, Solomon and Job.

Nor was Chaucer or his Latin predecessor the first to treat our poet as a source of edification. As early as the twelfth century, Hildebert of Tours, or one of his contemporaries, compiled a work entitled *Moralis Philosophia de Honesto et Utili,* which consists of brief definitions of various ethical terms followed by copious quotations from the ancient authors and the Bible. Ovid is cited, for instance, to show that

Venus and wine shatter the heart's ideals,

and this line from the *Fasti* is capped by a verse from *Ecclesiasticus.*[44] The " moral Senek " has his peer in the moral Naso. Humanists like John of Salisbury and Peter of Blois, scholastics like Alanus de Insulis and Roger Bacon, Vincent of Beauvais the encyclopaedist, John of Garland the educator, mystics like Hugo of St. Victor and Bernard of Clairvaux, His Holiness Pope Innocent III in his *De Contemptu Mundi,* — these and many more cite Ovid as an authority on morals and other sober subjects. Abelard takes counsel with *Ovidius Ethicus* in discussing monastic rules,

[132]

for the benefit of Eloise. He warns against excessive strictness, quoting from the *Amores:*

We strain at rules and crave what is forbidden.[45]

Eloise, on her part, in writing her lord and master of her disapproval of a common table for monks and nuns, adds that " even the poet of wantonness and teacher of turpitudes has shown in his *Book of Amatory Art* what chance for improper conduct is afforded by a banquet." Then follow six lines from the *Art of Love.*[46] Either Eloise had these verses at her tongue's end, or the volume itself was not far away. She knows its character well enough, and yet seeks its advice in a matter of morals, — *fas est et ab hoste doceri.*

To descend a moment into a later age, it is of some interest to note that Martin Luther wrote inside the cover of an edition of St. Anselm four verses of the *Amores,* one of them being that familiar line, veritably a winged word in the Middle Ages:

We strain at rules and crave what is forbidden.

Luther was not breaking monastic rules in jotting down these verses; he was paying tribute, in the traditional way, to *Ovidius Ethicus.* It is a pity that he was not more deeply read in Ovid; Erasmus had read to some profit.

Ovidius Theologus

If Ovid can give instruction in morals, it is no long step thence to theology. Again we find the starting-point for the excessive zeal of later interpreters in Ovid himself, in the unfeigned piety of the tale of Philemon and Baucis, in the apparent knowledge of the Old Testament displayed in his story of the Creation and the Flood, in the theistic modification of atomism likewise apparent in this story, in the philosophical competence of his Pythagorean solution presented in the last book of his cosmic epic. It was natural, then, that Ovid, like Virgil, should be subjected to the same spell of allegory that was cast over all literature, all art, and all natural phenomena in the Middle Ages; it was a universal reading of life.

With the twelfth century, this new interpretation is perfected into a science. A certain Johannes reveals in his versified *Integumenta* the secrets concealed in the *Metamorphoses*. A typical specimen of his ingenuity is his interpretation of the tale of Mars and Venus, detected in their amour by the jealous Vulcan.

Vulcan is Summer, Venus is the Spring;
Vile Mars, the Fall, doth alien bounties bring.

Whatever the appositeness of this glossing,
" the smartest scandal Heaven ever heard "
here becomes safe enough for any heaven. The
work of Johannes is only one of many allegorical commentaries written on the *Metamorphoses* in the twelfth century, still reposing,
unpublished, on library shelves. One exposition,
doubtless appreciated, was prepared *in usum
nonnarum;* nuns read Ovid moralized but not
expurgated, — really a more courteous way to
treat the poor pagan, and the poor nun.

In the thirteenth century, the moralization of
Ovid's tales becomes most elaborate. Chrétien
Legouais subjects the *Metamorphoses* to a
three-fold explanation: historical, moral and
theological. The story of Apollo and Daphne,
for instance, is interpreted in five different
ways. According to the last of these, Daphne
is the Blessed Virgin, loved by God, the real
sun of the world. When Apollo crowns himself
with laurel, it is God enveloping himself with
the body of that which he has made his mother.
Verily, the force of supernature can no further
go. No less profound is the moralization of the

poem written by Petrus Berchorius (Berçuire).
It is only Book 75 of his *Reductorium Morale,*
a gigantic work begun at Avignon and finished
at Paris in 1342. While at Avignon, he turned
for various bits of information to Petrarch,
whose passion for allegory was not what one
might expect of the "first modern man."

After the foregoing specimens of allegorical
ingenuity, we need not be surprised to find
Ovid actually quoted as Holy Writ. King
James I of Aragon (1218–1276) declares in his
Chronicle,[47] that at an assembly of the Bishops
and the Barons of his realm, he " rose and
began a text of Scripture:

' To *keep is no less virtue than to learn.'* "

If we are disposed to smile because the verse
comes from the *Art of Love* (ii. 13), we should
first ask ourselves whether we have ever heard
the maxim about tempering the wind to the
shorn lamb, — the utterance of a somewhat
Ovidian author — attributed to the Bible.
Ovid's line had acquired a similarly proverbial
character; it had appeared in the *Moralis Philosophia* of Hildebert.

The story of Ovid the theologian is an example of a perfectly natural process which goes

[136]

on in any age. To the age itself, such adaptation seems a brilliant and a modern affair; to coming generations it seems quaint. The author in his posthumous existence is simply adjusting himself to his new environment; he is a chameleon, exercising the art of protective coloring. The condition of Ovid in an age of allegorical interpretation is no more ridiculous than that of Virgil in a century of *Wissenschaft*.

Ovidius Medicus

Ovid's *Remedia Amoris* served a practical purpose in the Mediaeval schools; it was a text-book in both Latin and ethics. Nor was it treated less seriously by competent physicians. For instance, Arnaldus de Villa Nova, a great medical scholar (1240–1311), in discussing the lover's malady, *herosis*, takes more than one of his cures for amatory frenzy from Ovid. The patient should get to work, occupy his mind with some useful pursuit, seek a change of scene, enlist in the army, and rule his madness by dividing it among several sweethearts. For all these precepts, chapter and verse are cited from Ovid; he is an authority. Finally, Arnaldus calls in a hag, *vetula turpissima*, who

[137]

displays the imperfections of the mistress in a way even more revolting than they are set forth either in Ovid or in the Mediaeval *Vetula*. If the lover can stand such a disclosure, Arnaldus declares, he must be not a man but a devil incarnate, and may be abandoned to eternal perdition.

Ovidius Magus

The career of Master Virgil, the Magician, has something of a counterpart in Ovid's posthumous history. Strange stories clustered about his memory, as is natural enough in the case of any great man. We hear of two students who paid a visit to his tomb and asked his ghost what was the best of all his verses. The answer promptly came:

Virtue will even shun permitted joys.

This sentiment is Helen's, in her reply to Paris. The answer to the second question, what was the poet's worst, is no less satisfactory. The lines recanted by the poet come from Phaedra's epistle:

Pleasure is truth, truth pleasure. Jove says so:
'Tis all he knows, and all he needs to know.

Having compassion on the repentant heathen,

the young men offered prayers in his behalf.
At that there came a voice from the tomb:

> No *paternosters, I pray;*
> *Traveler, go on your way.*

The peasants about Sulmona know wilder
tales than this. Ovid, "Uiddiu," as they call
him, learned magic arts in the mystic grove of
the sorceress near Lucco. In one night he put
up a splendid villa, surrounded by gardens,
vineyards and orchards, and watered by a
spring which still is called "The Fount of
Love." To punish the curiosity of sight-seers,
he changed the men into birds, and the maidens
into a long line of poplars. When the terrified
inhabitants prayed his mercy, he mounted a
great chariot with horses of fire, and dashed
off to Rome. There he plied his profession as
before, creating warriors from dragons' teeth,
giving life to statues, changing a woman's hair
to snakes, or her legs to a fish's tail. Finally,
the King's daughter fell in love with him and
he with her. But the King was obdurate, and
sent the conjurer away to Siberia, a land of
perpetual snow. There the wizard died. But
he still visits his villa, and every Saturday night
he goes off with the witches to the nut-tree of
Benevento.

Here is a curious weaving of popular fancy about the tales of the *Metamorphoses*. Once Ovid's stories were let loose by some cleric, the good people of Sulmona could readily have attached them to the poet himself, along with other marvels. This process may indicate that the stories about Virgil the magician were more largely a product of Italian fancy than Comparetti, in his famous work, *Virgil in the Middle Ages,* would admit. Travellers like Conrad of Querfurt and Gervasius of Tilbury were not altogether wild-eyed barbarians; they may have exaggerated what they heard in Italy, but they doubtless heard wonders in plenty.

Ovid, along with his magic, is the hero of various amorous adventures, one of which, a famous one, had been told of Virgil. At the same time, Ovid is a very holy man, and numbered among the prophets of the coming of our Lord. Somewhat later than our period — in fact in the full flush of the sixteenth century — Ovid passed, with little difficulty, from magic to alchemy. Nicholas Valois composed in French verses a work, finished by the priest Vicot, entitled *Le Grande Olympe,* in which he sets forth for the first time, he declares, the true meaning of the stories of the *Metamor-*

phoses. Ovid's text is made a quarry for the alchemist's pick and shovel. He strikes gold immediately and constantly. The fable of Deucalion and Pyrrha, for instance, betokens, like the twin peaks of Parnassus, the masculine and the feminine elements among the metals, that is, gold and silver, from the union of which the philosopher's stone is produced. In this fashion, the whole poem is subjected to the fatal touch of Midas; Ovid's gold is converted into the baser metal. This sort of interpretation must have had something of a history before Valois and Vicot; one of their authorities was Arnaldus de Villa Nova, who was as learned in alchemy as we have found him in medicine.

Ovid's Alter Ego

After Virgil's fame was overgrown with magical accretions, a new personage came into being, utterly unlike his historical counterpart; his biography, separately recorded, touches the experience of our Virgil at hardly a single point. Ovid's personality did not quite double itself in this way, though there is material enough to form a lengthy and exciting career for an *alter Ovidius*. A good approach is made

by certain commentators of the twelfth century, who explain the poet's exile by his refusal
to accede to the amorous proposals of the Emperor's wife, who then, indignant at this slight,
falsely accused him to her husband. Livia in
the rôle of Potiphar's wife and Ovid in that of
Joseph, or Joseph Andrews, is indeed a novelty.
Possibly the full history of Ovid's double may
be discovered after all. A German poet of the
thirteenth century who continues the *Chronicle*
of Rudolf of Ems gives at least the outline of
such a story.[48]

> A *heathen known to fame*
> H*ad Ovid for his name.*
> A *writer of some note,*
> ' *The Tale of Troy' he wrote.*
> F*ar in a foreign land,*
> T*here ruled a monarch grand.*
> He *knew nor shame nor fear;*
> H*is virtues had no peer.*
> He *made Ovidius*
> H*is Chancellarius*
> A*nd his chief scribe. The lay*
> S*ays that one fatal day*
> T*o wrath the monarch stirred*
> W*hat from his Queen he heard.*
> S*o to avenge his wife,*
> H*e sought the poet's life.*

The King's method was to set Ovid adrift in a ship, first granting his request for a supply of pens, paper and parchment. On the voyage, Ovid wrote his *Tale of Troy*, and, on landing, sent back the book to the King. The King, who took a lively interest in the Trojan legend, pardoned the poet, and the work was translated from heathen Latin into good German.

viii. DANTE AND CHAUCER

At the end of the Mediaeval period, its two greatest writers, Dante and Chaucer, reflect in their different mirrors all that is most typical of the age. Both of them inevitably include in their picture of life something of what Ovid was and of what he had become.

Dante

For Dante, Ovid is one of the great world-poets, one of those whom with Virgil, his good guide, he meets in the pleasant greensward that delights the reader, somewhat unexpectedly, in the Limbo of Hell; Homer, Horace and Lucan are the other members of this tranquil group, and Statius greets the two travellers in Purgatory. Dante's reading of Ovid is shown by the most diverse sorts of reminiscences, which are more abundant than those of any Latin poet except Virgil. The spirit of Ovid the lover, chastened and refined, comes to Dante through the troubadours and the singers of the *dolce stil nuovo;* it is exalted, in the lyrics of the *Vita Nuova* and the *Convivio* and finally in the divine allegory of the *Commedia,* to heights of which Ovid never dreamed.

To *Ovidius Ethicus,* Dante appeals when discoursing, in the spirit of Juvenal, on true nobility.[49] Nor does Dante, supported by the allegorizing tendencies of his day, fail to find in the *Metamorphoses* a treasury of hidden meanings. With *Ovidius Magus* he has no concern, save with the magician who can set a metamorphosis before our eyes. To him he flings the challenge of a rival in his art. As he describes the simultaneous transformation of the robber Brunelleschi into the form of a serpent and of the serpent into the form of Brunelleschi, he exclaims:[50]

" Let Ovid be silent concerning Cadmus and Arethusa, for if, poetizing, he converts him into a serpent and her into a fountain, I envy him not; for two natures front to front never did he transmute, so that both the forms were prompt to exchange their matter." (NORTON)

This is a gauntlet too heavy for Ovid to raise. His magic is legerdemain. We admire the dexterity with which he deludes us, but we are conscious of the trick and of the performer's consciousness of it. When Dante tells the tale, we bow before a miracle.

Chaucer

If Ovid hardly touched the spirit of Dante, he contributed profoundly to the development of Chaucer's genius; Chaucer and Jean de Meun are the most conspicuous reincarnations of Ovid in the Middle Ages. Their temperaments are their own, but Ovid dwells within them. Chaucer, like Dante, names Ovid among the great poets of old,

Virgile, Ovyde, Omer, Lucan and Stace,[51]

and, it is safe to say, owes him a greater debt than to any other poet, old or new.

Chaucer learned Ovid in the writings of French masters, especially Jean de Meun and Guillaume de Machaut, and he also read him at first hand. His earlier works are packed with

[145]

Ovidian matter, nicely adjusted to his own design. In the new *Aeneid* which adorns the walls of the Temple of Venus in his *House of Fame*, Dido is drawn after Ovid rather than Virgil, and the epic itself is what Virgil's poem would be if it filtered through the *Art of Love*. One of the pillars in the House of Fame is erected to

> *V*enus clerk, Ovyde,
> T*hat hath y-sowen wonder wyde*
> T*he grete god of Loves name.*

Chaucer is professedly Ovid's pupil in the art of love, and he deeply understands the master's teaching.

Chaucer has also studied the nature of woman with Ovid's help, as is obvious in *Troilus*. The plan of the *Legend of Good Women* no less than much of its matter was furnished by Ovid. Ovid, as we have seen, had taken up the cudgels for the injured race in the third book of his *Art of Love*. Chaucer's defence is presented with the same enthusiasm and the same delicious undertone of irony.

In the *Canterbury Tales,* Chaucer fulfils a prophecy implicit in the *House of Fame* and fills his stage not with characters drawn from books but with the men and women of his own times, the "neyghebores" at his door. His debt to Ovid in this achievement is, at first sight, less conspicuous than before. Allusions and borrowings are far less abundant than in the earlier works. He has transcended Ovid, the singer of the tender loves, and now enters the list against Ovid the master of narrative and of a novel sort of epic. Though the subjects of the *Metamorphoses* and the *Canterbury Tales* have nothing in common, they are both collections of diverse stories which the authors would weave into a harmonious pattern. Chaucer did not finish his design, but that design, we may be sure, would have exhibited in the whole as it does in the parts a dexterity that matches Ovid's in securing variety, contrast, shifting of the scenes, unity in diversity and a self-concealing art.

The prevailing tone of the *Canterbury Tales* is that of comedy, with seasonings of ribaldry, irony and banter; but Chaucer's comedy is not merely gay. It is true to the full and ancient idea of comedy, the mirror of life, and has place for pathos, which may also deepen into tragedy. In "the Knight's Tale" and that of "the Man of Law," we have two stories appropriate for romance, one Classical and one

Mediaeval in matter, but both touched with tragedy and with the sublime simplicity of what Matthew Arnold called the grand style. Ovid has these tragic moments in his epic of transformations; both he and Virgil may have guided Chaucer, here and in *Troilus,* in his ennobling of romance. Chaucer's deeper moods are more intense than Ovid's and his art of dramatic portrayal is more vivid and diversified. Dryden praises them both, adding that " the figures in Chaucer are much more lively, and set in a better light." [52]

One turns back from Chaucer to Ovid with a deeper understanding of the latter's astounding combination of witty blasphemy and devotion to the sacred rite. Chaucer treats the Friar and the Sumner, both representatives of Holy Church, as cavalierly as Ovid does Jove and Apollo. The mediaeval poet could give points to Luther and even Erasmus for a more effective ridicule than theirs. But we turn from satire to the gentle piety of the Prioress, who tells of a miracle that awes the company, Miller and Sumner and all, into silence. There is pure religion and undefiled in the tale of Griselda, and the heart of the Christian faith is in the simple verses:

But hye god som tyme sendon can
His grace in-to a litel oxes stalle.

It is the hut of Philemon and Baucis once more, save that Chaucer, though no ardent mystic, is, as ever, deeper than Ovid when he sets his mind on serious things.

The *Canterbury Tales,* then, in which the poet might seem to have forgotten Ovid, show just as clearly the presence of notable Ovidian qualities, absorbed by Chaucer into his own temperament and art. Above all, the two poets are akin in their detachment of spirit. They have the liberated mind, not that of the sceptic like Anatole France, not that of the prophet, like Dante or Virgil, immersed in the world of ideas to which their art gives form, but that of Shakespeare, sympathetic of human follies and virtues and wisdoms and imaginings, yet disentangled from them. Horace is of this brotherhood, but in Ovid and Chaucer *nil admirari* has become a cosmic principle. Ovid, the whole Ovid, never was better understood than in the Ages of Faith, and no one ever so lived him through as Geoffrey Chaucer.

2. OVID IN THE RENAISSANCE

THE Renaissance was another *aetas Ovidiana*. At what time Ovid " returned " it were hard to say, for he had never departed. But antiquity as a whole was more zealously sought and found in this tremendous period than in the centuries preceding — the term " Renaissance " is no misnomer. Ovid's popularity, as attested by translations, allusions and imitations in the literature of all the European countries, was securely established and ever enlarged its bounds. The thirst for ancient life and thought found satisfaction in his pages. Painters and sculptors no less than poets, turned to the *Metamorphoses* for stories and themes, and for pictures that needed only the transferring to canvas or to stone. His work became an authoritative Bible of Art.

i. PETRARCH AND BOCCACCIO

Petrarch reckoned Ovid among his favorites. With a hint from the *Amores,* he hit on an invention in his *Trionfo d'Amore* that enjoyed a wide vogue in contemporary and subsequent poetry. But no *censor morum* could be more savage than Petrarch in berating the indecency of that " insane work," the *Art of Love,* worthy cause of the poet's exile, and typical product of a mind " lascivious, lecherous, and altogether mulierous." In general, Petrarch is too serious and self-centred to make Ovid his friend for life.

Boccaccio started with an intensely intimate friendship with Ovid. His early works, both Latin and Italian, are saturated with the amorosities of Ovid's early poetry and with the gay fancy of the *Metamorphoses.* In *Fiametta,* he has constructed an elaborate tissue from the *Heroides* and added his darling to their number. Ovid, praised by name, has furnished many of the " ensamples olde " for the *Amorosa Visione,* but here the spirit of Corinna is caught up into that of Beatrice and of Laura. The pastoral fairy-land of *Ameto* takes much of its scenery from the *Metamorphoses.* We cannot deny that Boccaccio, or Sannazaro after him, may have known something of the Greek romance, but for the essence of the *Ameto* or the *Arcadia,* we need look no further than Ovid, Virgil, a few other Romans, and the genius of the two authors. In the *Decamerone,* Boccaccio, like Chaucer, essays a larger contest with Ovid. If with Dryden, we allow Chaucer a special

prize as master of drama, the three contestants all come off with flying colors, — *Arcades
omnes*.

In the latter half of his bisected life, spent
soberly under the spell of the worshipped
Petrarch, Boccaccio turned to Ovid chiefly for
material for his scholarly work *De Genealogia
Deorum;* Virgil is his principal authority, with
Ovid a close second. Boccaccio is not, like
Chaucer and Jean de Meun, an Ovid perfected
and transcended, but an *Ovide manqué*. In his
youth, Ovid somewhat went to his head, and
in his old age was somewhat banished from his
heart.

ii. NEO-LATIN POETRY

As the full flush of the Renaissance comes
on, Latin poetry grows into a new art, beside
which the Latin verse of Dante, and even that
of Petrarch and Boccaccio, seemed to critics
of the day primitive and crude. In the work of
its best representatives, such as Pontano and
Sannazaro, this poetry is no mere learned exercise, but an expression of the writer's temperament no less genuine than his writings in
his mother-tongue. To know fully the mind of
any poet of the age — and the age includes

John Milton — we must not relegate his Latin poems to an appendix, but read them in order with his other works.

Ovid's influence appears chiefly in the elegies of the period; it notably affected their form. The idea of love, as we have seen, that Ovid sets forth in his early poems, was refined and etherealized as it passed into the Mediaeval Knightly Code and the poetry of the Troubadors, whence it was exalted to heights yet more sublime by Dante and, following in his wake, by Petrarch and Boccaccio; Boccaccio's *Amorosa Visione* presents these three stages in turn. Later in the Renaissance, the spirit of Ovid reasserts itself. But Plato, too, was a sovereign influence from the days of the Florentine Academy, and these two battle hard for the soul of every poet of the coming centuries who sang of love. The " Platonism " of Spenser and the " metaphysical " school in English poetry is strongly seasoned with Ovid; at last his influence quite faded away in the purer idealism of Wordsworth's ode.

Of the two writers whom I have selected as representative of the best in Neo-Latin poetry, Pontano reflects in his verse the gorgeous colorings of the bay of Naples, whose islands and peaks and inlets he transformed, with a fresh sense of myth, into nymphs and deities and subjects for his poems. Pontano's most original use of the elegy is in his *De Amore Coniugali*. Ovid might be mystified at such a title, but would admire the contents; for this proper poet has more sensuous charm and passion than any of the Roman poets of love, with the single exception of Catullus. The initial poem of the third book is in homage of Ovid. Pontano stands raptly gazing on the town of the poet's birth, and imagines a meeting between Ovid and Corinna there. A dialogue ensues in which Ovid in the rôle of the passionate shepherd is seriously intense for once.

Sannazaro is a gentler spirit, more celestial than Pontano; his verse has less color and more grace. When he imitates Ovid in swearing fidelity to his mistress, his oath is true. When he takes the lament for Tibullus as a model for his eulogy of Pontano, he avoids witty incongruities and utters his devotion simply. Sannazaro no less than his friend has the art of peopling the hills and streams about Naples with sprightly personifications. This is the charm of his famous invention in the pastoral, his *Fisher Eclogues:* Virgilian in form, they have many a coloring from Ovid. In the *Sal-ices,* he tells of the escape of some nymphs from a troop of villain satyrs and their merci-ful transformation into willows, which still shrink from the touch of their pursuers and lean far out across the stream. Catullus could not surpass the grace or Ovid the narrative rapidity of this perfect little poem.

Ovidius Ethicus was not forgotten in the Renaissance. Commentaries were written as explicitly moral as those of the twelfth century. Ovid is also the starting-point for a long line of " Sacred Fasti," beginning with " good old Mantuan " in 1513 and continued by French writers of Latin verse like the Benedictine Hugo Vaillant (1674). Similarly, the *Art of Love* was translated into something supernal. Petrus Iacobus Martellus in 1698 published at Bologna his *L'Arte d'Amar Dio,* and Thomas Ravasinus at Paris in 1706 two books *De Arte Amandi S. Mariam.*

For a typical utterance of what Ovid meant in the Renaissance, we may consult the edition by Guido Morillonius in 1516. This scholar declares:

" When, not many days ago, I would re-fresh my mind after the meanderings of the dialecticians and seek the holy dwellings of the Muses, by chance I laid hand on the *Heroides* of Ovid. Ye Gods, what manifold learning do they display, and how they twinkle with sprightly wit! If Horace gave his vote for one who could combine the profitable and the pleasant, none, methinks, can excel Ovid in this art. He has so mingled the serious with honey-sweet fiction and fiction with the serious, that 'tis hard telling whether he offers us more pleasure than profit or more profit than pleasure."

Such was the agreeable compound discovered by most readers at that time in the works of Ovid.

3. OVID IN MODERN POETRY

IN THE wide expanse of modern literature, it were profitless to enumerate every author who has in some fashion drawn inspiration from Ovid's poetry. From the Renaissance to the Romantic movement at the close of the eighteenth century, Ovid's works were firmly fixed in the programme of liberal studies. It were difficult to mention a writer of eminence in the literatures of Europe who showed no acquaintance with Ovid in writing on Ovid's themes. Modern reincarnations of Ovid occur, though none so impressive as Jean de Meun or Chaucer. There is no greater treat for a lover of literature than to master an ancient poet, Homer or Euripides, Virgil or Ovid, and to read through those moderns who studied him best.

In Italian literature, for example, we turn to Ariosto. He is replete with reminiscences of Ovid, but to recognize these is only the beginning of the reader's interest. We must know the background of Ariosto, first of all, by following the course of the Mediaeval chivalrous epic as it is reinterpreted by Pulci and Boiardo, and by noting the Classical flavors with which these romances, like those of the Middle Ages, were spiced. The spirit of Ovid is more obvious in Pulci and that of Virgil in Boiardo. We are then ready for the *Orlando Furioso,* which will furnish the Ovidian reader unbounded entertainment. The poem is a glorious mixture, a whirlwind of adventures and magic, flying dragons, enchanted castles and furious combats. The magic is not that of Ovid, made natural by the poet's sleight-of-hand, nor that of Dante, made true by the poet's faith, — it is a slap, dash, devil-may-care magic which recks not of reason or credulity. The work is a kaleidoscope of all history, all cultures, all beliefs, with a riot of Ovidian irony and burlesque. Woe to the critic, if he would avoid the madhouse, who would plot Ariosto's epic technique! Not only the hero but the epic is *furioso,* and the reader is mad with delight.

In Portuguese literature, we shall find a wide acquaintance with Ovid exhibited by Camoens in his famous epic, *Lusiadas.* Turning to Spain, we observe Ovid assisting at the inception of the modern novel. The *Comedia de Calisto y Melibea,* known as the *Celestina,* written at the close of the fifteenth century, owes its general plot to Ovid's amatory poems and to the Mediaeval *Pamphilus.* In form, it is a prose dialogue, which holds in solution both the novel and the drama. In the drama, we shall find a thorough student of Ovid in Lope de Vega. In the work of which he himself was most fond, the *Dorotea,* he harks back to *Celestina* for the character of the go-between, but besides this, the piece is crowded with reminiscences of Ovid. Calderon appreciated the " serious relief " furnished by the story of Cephalus and Procris in the *Art of Love* and the *Metamorphoses,* for he made a tragedy of it in his *Celos aun del Aire Matan*. He also saw that it made good stuff for comedy, and turned it into one, his *Céfalo y Procris*. These examples will suffice to convince the Ovidian that his poet was well known to Spanish writers. To meet Ovid's peer in narrative irony and burlesque, one has only to turn to Cervantes.

Erasmus gives us the best of Holland, and the *Praise of Folly* is Erasmus at his best. The satire is essentially Horatian, with a bit of Lucian thrown in, yet the reader of Ovid will feel that he is breathing a familiar air. In Germany, we may strike at once for the highest, for Ovid is one of the Latin poets whom Goethe greatly relished. As is plain from *Dichtung und Wahrheit*, he had read Ovid at an early age, and later he defended him against Herder's attacks. There are constant reminiscences of Ovid in *Wilhelm Meister*. When Goethe took his departure from Rome in 1781, his own distress of mind recalled to him Ovid's farewell to his city in the *Tristia*, and prompted the writing of the *Römische Elegien*. We should not expect much of Ovid in *Faust*, — except perhaps in the person of Mephistopheles — and yet Goethe pays homage to his beloved poet by inserting Philemon and Baucis among the manifold figures in his great vision of life at the end of the poem.

Ovid is more at home in France than in Germany. He is a favorite with the authors of the *Pleiade,* — Marot, Baïf, DuBellay and Ronsard. Montaigne read him at school on the sly. The satires of Régnier contain many close imitations of Ovid. One of them reproduces the libertine's confession of *Amores,* ii. 4; as Régnier is not a libertine but a moralist, his poem is tinged with virtuous longings and regrets, — it is a new sort of *Ovide moralisé.* Still, Régnier could imitate in another style. Later in the seventeenth century, translations of our poet multiplied; La Fontaine turned the *Metamorphoses* into *rondeaux.* As *praeceptor amoris* Ovid assumed in polite society the authority that he had once exercised in the Mediaeval Courts of Love. He furnished many subjects for drama and opera. Above all, Molière should be read from cover to cover by the true Ovidian, not merely for the abundant imitations, but for the spirit of comedy of which he and Ovid and the few elect who are chronicled in Meredith's essay know the inner secrets. The atmosphere of *Carmina Amatoria* is constantly about us in Molière's plays. In his *Amphitryon,* for instance, he has avoided Plautus's daring combination of divine burlesque and divine worship; the comedy of the gods at the beginning of the play is in the manner not of Plautus but of Ovid.

Ovid, the master of burlesque, was himself subjected to that irreverence. Following in the wake of Scarron's new *Aeneid,* D'Assoucy turned the myths of the *Metamorphoses* into travesty. Ovid would not have been shocked, though he might wonder at the necessity of such performances. All in all, the seventeenth century in French literature is another *aetas Ovidiana.* In fact, it may well be that the qualities which impress us today as distinctively French were at least partly due to the deliberate study of antique models, first during the régime of the *Pleiade,* at the beginning of the sixteenth century, and again, with special devotion to Ovid, in the times of the Grand Monarque. Courtesy, finesse and style —virtues conspicuously French—would surely be recognized in Ovid and be fortified by his example.

Ovid's prestige suffered no diminution in the eighteenth century, as the names of Gentil-

Bernard and André Chénier will serve to suggest. In an elegy on the exile of the poet, Lingendes scorches the barbarian Augustus for robbing his country of the rarest spirit that it had ever seen. He consoles the exile with the hospitality that France extends and with the French beauties, *la belle Renée* in particular, whose like the city of Aeneas never saw. So then, he exclaims:

Va *trouver les Français où le destin t'appelle*
  Pour *finir ton malheur,*
Et *quitte de bon coeur ta langue maternelle*
  Pour *apprendre la leur.*

But Ovid had been speaking French — and the French Ovidian — for some time.

Even during the Romantic revolt, our poet was too French to be permanently cast aside. In the year VII of that New Era which the Disciples of Reason established for mankind, though less solidly than they supposed, there was printed in Paris, " sous les yeux et par les soins de " J. C. Poncelin, a translation into French of the *Oeuvres Complettes d'Ovide,* accompanied in the different volumes by exquisite engravings, one of which, reproduced above, represents a not altogether heart-broken Ovid in exile. Since the Romantic movement, French scholarship has made admirable contributions to our understanding of Ovid, but among men of letters, few besides Banville and Anatole France may be numbered among his disciples. The appearance of a golden little volume on Ovid by Emile Ripert marks, let us hope, the beginning of a better era.

In our own literature, after Chaucer and Gower, we may meet Ovid again in the graceful fancies of Spenser's *Faerie Queene* and find a new pastoral *Fasti* in his *Shephearde's Calendar*. There are suggestions of Corinna in Sidney's Stella, though the poet had no need to fear the reproach " That Plato I have reade for nought." A new sort of *Heroides* is invented by Drayton, who composes, in his *England's Heroical Epistles,* message and answer for Rosamund and Henry II, Queen Katherine and Owen Tudor, and other noble (and rather heavy) characters. In the Elizabethan drama, Ovid supplies subjects for many of the mythological plays, including the daring use of the story of Iphis and Ianthe in the *Maid's Metamorphosis,* an anonymous piece written about 1600. One will discover many a bit of Ovid by browsing about in Heywood and Lyly and

Peele. In Lyly's *Endimion,* when Sir Tophas falls in love with a very Ovidian character, the " old enchantress," Dipsas, he reels off Latin quotations, mostly from the *Art of Love,* and says to his servant: " Epi, I feel all Ovid *de arte amandi* lie as heavie at my heart as a loade of logges." Ben Jonson, who has not so many borrowings from Ovid as one might expect, constructs a sub-plot in the *Poetaster* from the poet's life.

" As the soul of Euphorbus was thought to live in Pythagoras," said Francis Meres, in his *Palladis Tamia,* " so the sweet witty soul of Ovid lives in mellifluous and honey-tongued Shakespeare." Shakespeare is another of our poet's reincarnations. There is hardly an aspect of Ovid's genius and art that one will not see reproduced somewhere in Shakespeare. Ovid's works are a storehouse of ancient lore for him, and a monument of " the elegancy and golden cadence of poesy." Naso he is indeed, the man " for smelling out the odoriferous flowers of fancy, the jerks of invention." [53] But primarily, it is the call of deep unto deep that Shakespeare hears in Ovid. A brilliant essayist of our day finds in Shakespeare, as many have found in Ovid, a lack of religion. [54]

This analysis leaves something unexplained, and yet both spirits are free, looking about on a world of shifting circumstance, and moulding it into what their fancy wills.

The youthful Milton, Puritan though he was, consecrated his earliest verse to Ovid. Curious evidence of his fondness for Ovid has recently come to light, in the shape of one hundred and seventy-one stanzas written by Milton at the age of fifteen to accompany a set of drawings illustrating scenes in the *Metamorphoses*. The juvenile phrases here exhibited may be traced in the poet's later works.[55] Milton's Latin verse, free and convivial in some of its specimens, must be read simultaneously with the *Ode on the Nativity, Lycidas* and the other English poems, if we would see the conflict of Ovid and Virgil in Milton's mind and art.[56] Ovid leads at the start, but Virgil wins, and becomes the poet's foremost model in *Paradise Lost*. Yet Ovid is not flung aside. He furnishes Milton with matter and with devices, both of which are sublimated in the loftier Virgilian air of his epic.

The poetry, both the gay and the sober, of Herrick and Cowley will take on new meaning if one come to them fresh from Ovid. Dryden's

satire will be found more nearly akin to Ovid
than to the other ancient models that he so
nicely balances in his essay. In his *Fables,* he
has, perhaps unconsciously, summed up the
course of Mediaeval narrative by selecting as
his typical raconteurs Chaucer, Boccaccio and
Ovid. As master of the stage, Dryden passed
on his sceptre to Congreve, and in Congreve,
Ovid, the Ovid of the *Art of Love,* lives again.
There has never been a finer monument to
Ovid's placid irony than the *Way of the World.*
Gay and Prior are worthy masters of Ovid's
comedy. Swift's satire is more bitter, Pope's is
of sharper tang and Addison is a gentler spirit.
And yet the reader of Ovid will find his mas-
ter's presence in them all.

The Romantic movement in England, as in
the other countries of Europe, sounds Ovid's
knell, though not for Byron, who, as author of
Don Juan, often suggests the flavor of Pope.
We should not view Romanticism too narrowly,
for Landor, a discreet admirer of Ovid, lived
through the period, and Shelley carried his
copy of our poet as he travelled about in Italy.
Amongst the Victorians, Tennyson shows some
reading of our poet, particularly in *Oenone,* and
Browning's omnivorous appetite finds satisfac-

tion now and then in the marvels of the *Metamorphoses* or the poet's romantic career. Swinburne, whose masters are the Greeks, had studied Ovid for his *Atalanta*. But despite such incidental homage, Ovid had had his day. This was no *aetas Ovidiana*, and none has followed since. It is perhaps about time that our poet's star should once more take the ascendant.

III. OVID THE MODERN

" Les anciens, monsieur, sont les anciens, et nous sommes
les gens de maintenant."

MOLIÈRE

Prisca iuvent alios, ego me nunc denique natum
  Gratulor: haec aetas moribus apta meis.

OVID

" En vérité Ovide est encore, en ce debut du XXe siècle,
un poète d'actualité."

RIPERT

TWO eminent authorities on Dante have
declared:
  " It would hardly be an exaggeration
to say that distinctly modern literature has its
springs in the French poets of the twelfth century, and that these poets were inspired and
(paradox as it may seem) ' modernized ' by the
inspiration they drew from Ovid." [57]
  There is nothing paradoxical here, for Ovid
is a modern of the moderns. It is curious how
we change our views about modernity as we
push back our studies into the past. We begin
by setting the highest values on things modern.
We rightly reject what is antiquated and mean-
ingless in favor of what is contemporary and

real. Then, by chance, we discover something that immediately concerns us in Thucydides or Plato or Horace, and we say: " How modern these ancients were!" At the time when they wrote, they thought themselves modern too. If they can speak to us today, they are more alive than one whose heart and lungs are still in operation, but whose brain perished centuries ago. As our studies proceed and the writers of old seem more and more like human beings, all of a sudden our perspective is reversed, as when the planetary system of Ptolemy changed to that of Copernicus. History no longer revolves egocentrically about us; we begin to know our place in the shifting panorama of time. We no longer congratulate the ancients on being modern, but ourselves on our new-found ability to appreciate living thought by whomsoever it has been expressed. Literature has taught us how to tell the quick from the dead. We embark on a voyage of discovery, prepared to make ourselves contemporary with the best of the past, and to recognize modernity wherever there is life.

To be contemporary with every age, a writer must, first of all, seem modern to his own. One whose imagination is fed merely by the past, one who believes that the count of mighty poets is made up and the scroll of them folded in the Muse's hands, has, to the best of his ability, sounded the death-knell of his own poetry. The root of his fancy is strong, but the flower is weak. Unless, like Keats, he belies his words in his practice, he will soon be swept aside by the living thought of his times. Something is lacking in his sanity and in his sense of humor, if he cannot exclaim with our poet:

> Let *others praise the hoary past. But how*
> I *thank my stars I was not born till now!*
> *The present age is suited to my ways.*[58]

To understand our debt to Ovid, we may, to be sure, follow the course of his posthumous fame and the manner of his appeal to the different ages. Irrespective of his own attainments, we must ever be grateful to the writer who saved for literature the stories of Midas, of Alcyone, of Atalanta's race, of Pyramus and Thisbe, of Philemon and Baucis, — jewels that have sparkled in diverse settings of pure gold. We must also acknowledge the genius of a writer who invented a new literary form like the *Heroides* that proved prolific of emulation in most of the subsequent periods of literature.

But it is even more essential to know the man himself and his art. We owe a debt only to those who can speak to our own times. The Classics live today not because the ancient authors became famous, — *magnorum nominum umbrae* — but because they were modern.

Ovid was modern, first, in his art of interpreting the past in terms of his own age, in making his heroes Augustan, in pushing back the boundary of his times to include the first moments of history. It is the god Janus, once a shapeless mass in the sea of primeval chaos, who gives Ovid the maxim:

> We *praise old times but use the present age.*

Yet, after all, this is modernity in the less important sense; it accounts for the poet's popularity in his life-time but not for his appeal to posterity. Ovid will remain modern so long as the universal qualities that make him great are valued by mankind, — his wit, his art, his creative fancy, the mastery of his own moods and of his plastic world. Wit was his ruin, but we may pardon its excess. The exile's misery is his atonement and perpetually a moral for soberminded folk to draw. It is profitable to draw the moral, yet we need not emblazon it forever in letters of lead, — *ingenio periit*. Fatal to him, his wit is no disaster to mankind, so long as a spark of comedy survives.

Nor does Ovid fail to give us that criticism of life which to Matthew Arnold is the essence of literature. Gilbert Murray, who has come nobly to Ovid's defence, finds, after all, that our poet's criticism of life is slight. It is such as is " passed by a child, playing alone and peopling the summer evening with delightful shapes, upon the stupid nurse who drags it off to bed." [59] I venture to see in Ovid a spirit more mature than this. His mimic world is no toy fancy, a thing apart. He rather has absorbed life into it as into the only verity that remains eternal amid the flux and flow. Ovid dwells in his mind rather than in the images that it creates. His thought is so little obtrusive, his art is so careful that we too hastily circumscribe its limits instead of stretching our own imaginations by its aid. Ovid perishes for his style — like Cicero among the philosophers — no less than for his wit.

As we glance back at the periods of history that have valued Ovid most, — that *aetas Ovidiana* in the Ages of Faith, the Renaissance in all the countries of Europe, the times of

Louis XIV in French literature, those of Elizabeth, the Restoration and Queen Anne — we become aware that these are very eminent periods in human civilization. The horrible thought may occur that possibly our own age, despite its triumphs in the natural sciences and in creature comforts, may somewhat have slipped from the heights of literary taste. We are a restless race, not having time to live even in the present, much less in the past. Would Ovid's ghost have again to exclaim, as in the darker part of the Middle Ages:

I'm barbarous here, whom none can understand?

Ovid was too modern for the Dark Age; perhaps he is too modern for ours. Who would think that? Away with such blasphemy! It is mere chance that our eyes have turned a blind spot towards Ovid. Books have their fates. How else could Meredith nicely describe the spirit of Ovid's comedy without mentioning his name? He could not have read him with care. Otherwise, he would have made Naso toast-master at his famous symposium on Noses in *Diana of the Crossways* and have raised his glass at Shakespeare's eulogy and Herrick's toast:

> A *Goblet next I'le drink*
> *To Ovid; and suppose*
> *Made he the pledge, he'd think*
> *The world had all one Nose.*[60]

The Dark Age had the disadvantage of not possessing Ovid's works. We who have erred can easily make amends. It is a comfortable penance; open his books and read.

NOTES AND BIBLIOGRAPHY

NOTES

1. F. L. Lucas, *Euripides and his Influence*, p. 69, Boston, 1923, in the Series, *Our Debt to Greece and Rome*.

2. *Controversiae*, ii. 2. 12.

3. *Tristia*, iv. 10. 53 ff.

4. *Amores*, iii. 15. 7.

5. *Tristia*, iv. 10. 59:
   Moverat ingenium totam cantata per urbem
   Nomine non vero dicta Corinna mihi.
   Tristia, ii. 427:
   Sic sua lascivo cantata est saepe Catullo
   Femina, cui falsum Lesbia nomen erat.

6. *Carmen*, 85.

7. *Tristia*, ii. 340.

8. Introduction to the *Annus Mirabilis* (ed. G. R. Noyes, p. 25).

9. *Voyage autour de ma Chambre,* chapter xxv.

10. *Romance of the Rose*, vv. 10692 ff. The edition of Michel is cited, as more generally accessible than the critical edition by Langlois.

11. *Romance of the Rose*, vv. 9090 ff. The whole passage shows a close study of Ovid.

12. In *"The Padlock."*

13. Ripert, *Ovide*, p. 43.

14. *House of Fame*, vv. 627 ff.

15. Sir James G. Frazer, with an English translation (in *The Loeb Classical Library*), ii. p. 394.

16. *Met.*, ii. 450 ff.

17. *Met.*, vii. 797 ff.

18. *Met.*, xii. 414 ff.

19. *Met.*, xii. 162 ff.

20. *Met.*, xv. 426 ff.

21. Herrick, "A Ternarie of Littles, upon a Pipkin of Jellie sent to a Lady," in his *Hesperides*.

22. *Fasti*, iii. 111 ff.

23. *De Rerum Natura*, ii. 600 ff.

24. *Met.*, i. 325 ff.

25. *Fasti*, iv. 331 ff.

26. *Fasti*, v. 297 ff.

27. *Fasti*, i. 201 ff.

28. *Fasti*, v. 681 ff.

29. *Odes*, iv. 5. 23.

30. *Epistulae*, ix. 4.

31. *Tristia*, i. 1. 39.

32. *Tristia*, iii. 4. 55 ff.

33. *Tristia*, v. 10. 37.

34. *Tristia*, iii. 3. 73 ff.

35. *Naturalis Historia*, xxxii. 152.

36. C. O. Minchin, *Sea Fishing; Ars Amatoria*, iii. 425.

37. *Fasti*, i. 493 ff.

38. *Ex Ponto*, ii. 10. 39 ff.

39. *Ex Ponto*, i. 2. 53:
    Sic ubi percepta est brevis et non vera voluptas,
    Peior ab admonitu fit status iste boni.
    See Dante, *Inferno*, v. 121 ff.

40. *Heroides*, xvi. 290; Juvenal, *Sat.*, x. 297.

41. The authorship of both the *Mathematicus* and the *Susanna* is in dispute.

42. G. L. Kittredge, "Chaucer's Lollius," in *Harvard Studies in Classical Philology*, XXVIII (1917).

43. *Fasti*, iii. 675 ff.

44. *Fasti*, i. 301, slightly changed by the compiler, but not to the injury of the sense; *Ecclesiasticus*, 19. 2: Vinum et mulieres apostatare faciunt sapientes.

45. *Amores*, iii. 4. 17:
    Nitimur in vetitum semper cupimusque negata.

46. *Ars Amatoria*, i. 233 ff.

47. Translated by John Forster, 1883, II. p. 507.

48. K. Bartsch, *Albrecht von Halberstadt und Ovid im Mittelalter*, pp. xii ff.

49. *Convivio*, iv. 15. 71.

50. *Inferno*, xxv. 97 ff.

51. *Troilus*, v. 1792.

52. *Preface to the Fables,* p. 743. Dryden's essay can be read again and again with profit by lovers of Ovid and Chaucer.

53. *Love's Labour's Lost,* iv. 2. 127.

54. G. Santayana, " The Absence of Religion in Shakespeare," in his *Interpretations of Poetry and Religion,* New York, 1900.

55. H. C. H. Candy, *Some Newly Discovered Stanzas written by John Milton on Engraved Scenes illustrating Ovid's Metamorphoses,* 1924.

56. See E. K. Rand, " Milton in Rustication," in *The University of North Carolina Studies in Philology,* XIX, 109–135 (1922).

57. P. H. Wicksteed and E. G. Gardner, *Dante and Giovanni del Virgilio,* Westminster, 1902, p. 316.

58. *Ars Amatoria,* iii. 121.

59. *Essays and Addresses,* 1921, in the essay on " Poesis and Mimesis." The pages on Ovid contain, in brief compass, some of the finest things that have been said of Ovid in years.

60. " To Live Merrily and to Trust to Good Verses," in his *Hesperides.*

The translations in this book are, unless otherwise specified by E. K. R.

BIBLIOGRAPHY

I. Essays and Books on Ovid.

ALLINSON, ANNE C. E., *Roads from Rome*. New York, 1913. (See chapter, " A Roman Citizen.")

BAILEY, C., *P. Ovidii Nasonis Fastorum Liber III*. Oxford, 1921. (See Editor's sketch of Roman religion.)

BRADFORD, G., " Ovid among the Goths," in *The Yale Review*, IV. 544–559 (1915).

DIMSDALE, M. S., *A History of Latin Literature*. New York, 1915.

DRYDEN, *Annus Mirabilis (Account of the Poem)*, *Discourse concerning the Original and Progress of Satire*, *Preface to the Fables*.

DUFF, J. W., *A Literary History of Rome from the Origins to the Close of the Golden Age*. London and New York, 1909, pp. 578 ff. (with an account of the chief editions of Ovid's works).

HAIGHT, ELIZABETH H., *Italy Old and New*. New York, 1922. (Chapter XV, " Ovid in Sulmona.")

KNAPP, C., " Helps to the Study of the *Metamorphoses* of Ovid," in *The Classical Weekly*, XVI. pp. 25 ff. (1922); XVII. pp. 65 ff. (1923) (articles, with descriptive bibliography).

LANDOR, W. S., *Imaginary Conversations of Greeks and Romans*. London, 1853. (" Tibullus and Messala " contains remarks on Ovid.)

MURRAY, G., *Tradition and Progress*. Boston, 1922. (See the essay on " Poesis and Mimesis," repeated from *Essays and Addresses*. London, 1921.)

NAGEOTTE, E., *Ovide, sa Vie, ses Oeuvres*. Dijon, 1872.

OWEN, S. G., " Ovid " in *The Encyclopaedia Britannica* [11], 1911. See also under III.

RAND, E. K., " Ovid and the Spirit of Metamorphosis," in *Harvard Essays on Classical Subjects*. Boston, 1912, pp. 207–38.

BIBLIOGRAPHY

RIPERT, É., *Ovide, Poète de l'Amour, des Dieux et de l'Exile*. Paris, 1921. (With an account of the influence of Ovid on French literature.)

SLATER, D. A., " Ovid in the Metamorphoses," in *Occasional Publications of the Classical Association*, No. 1, pp. 1–28. Cambridge, England [1914?].

SELLAR, W. Y., *The Roman Poets of the Augustan Age: Horace and the Elegiac Poets*. Oxford, 1899. (Chapter V, " Ovid.")

—— " Ovid," in *Encyclopaedia Britannica* 9, 1885. (With remarks on Ovid's influence on literature.)

SMITH, K. F., " The Poet Ovid," in *The University of North Carolina Studies in Philology*, XV. 307–332 (1918). Reprinted in Martial, *The Epigrammatist, and Other Essays*. Baltimore, 1920.

WHEELER, A. L.: see under II.

WRIGHT, F. A.: see under II.

II. Editions and Translations into English.

See KNAPP, under I.

Amores and *Heroides:*

Palmer, A. (editor), *Heroides*. Oxford, 1898. Shuckburgh, E. S. (editor), *Heroides*. London, 1896.

In *Verse*, Marlowe (*Amores*), Dryden, Pope and others; in *Prose*, Showerman, Grant, Translation with Latin text, in *The Loeb Classical Library*. New York, 1914.

Ars Amatoria

In *Verse*, Dryden, Congreve and others; Wright, F. A., *The Lover's Handbook*. London and New York, 1924. (In *The Broadway Translations*, with essays on the life and works of Ovid, his influence on English literature, and an account of previous translations of the *Art of Love* into English.)

Remedia Amoris

In *Prose*, Riley, H. T., in *The Bohn Library*. London, 1851–52.

Metamorphoses

In *Verse*, Golding (Shakespeare's *Ovid*), Sandys, Dryden, Pope and others; in *Prose*, Miller, F. J., Translation with Latin text, in *The Loeb Classical Library*. London and New York, 1916. (2 vols.)

Fasti

In *Verse*, Taylor, J. (the first four books), 1839; in *Prose*, Mongan, R., 1880. Peter, Hermann (editor), *P. Ovidi Nasonis Fastorum Libri VI*. Leipzig, 1907.

Ibis

Ellis, R. (editor), *Ibis*. Oxford, 1881.

In *Verse*, Jones, John, 1658.

Tristia & Ex Ponto

In *Prose*, Wheeler, A. L., Translation with Latin text and an introduction on Ovid's life and works, in *The Loeb Classical Library*. New York and London, 1924.

OWEN, S. G., *Tristia, Liber II* (edited with notes and an introduction on Ovid's life and works), 1923.

—— (editor), *P. Ovidi Nasonis Tristium Libri V*. Oxford, 1889.

III. Ovid's Influence on Later Literature.

COOPER, LANE, *The Greek Genius and its Influence*. New Haven, 1917. (General bibliography, pp. 281 ff.)

KNAPP, C., See under I.

OWEN, S. G., "Ovid and Romance," in *English Literature and the Classics*. Oxford, 1912. (Edited by G. S. Gordon.)

Ovid in Art:

BREDT, E. W., *Bilderschatz zur Weltliteratur. I. Ovid: der Götter Verwandlungen*. Munich [1922]. (Reproduction and explanation of important paintings inspired by descriptions in the *Metamorphoses*.)

IV. Ovid in the Middle Ages.

BARTSCH, K. F., *Albrecht von Halberstadt und Ovid im Mittelalter*. Quedlinburg, 1861.

BREUL, K., *The Cambridge Songs, A Goliard's Song Book of the XIth Century*. Cambridge, England, 1915.

BIBLIOGRAPHY

CONNELY, W., "Imprints of the *Heroides* of Ovid on Chaucer," in *The Classical Weekly*, XVIII. 9–13 (1924).

FARAL, E., *Recherches sur les Sources Latines des Contes et Romans Courtois du Moyen Age*. Paris, 1913.

—— *Les Arts Poétiques du XIIe et du XIIIe Siècle*. Paris, 1924.

GRAF, A., *Roma nella Memoria e nelle Immaginazioni del Medio Evo*. 2 vols. Torino, 1882–1883. Vol. II. pp. 296 ff.

KITTREDGE, G. L., *Chaucer and his Poetry*. Cambridge, Mass., 1915.

—— "Chaucer's Lollius," in *Harvard Studies in Classical Philology*, XXVIII. 49–133 (1917).

LANGLOIS, E., *Origines et Source du Roman de la Rose*. Paris, 1891.

LEHMANN, P., *Die Parodie im Mittelalter*. München, 1922.

—— *Parodistische Texte*. München, 1923.

LOWES, J. L., "The Loveres Maladye of Hereos," in *Modern Philology*, XI. 491–546 (1914). (For Ovidius Medicus.)

MACDONELL, ANNE, *In the Abruzzi*. London, 1908. (Chapter XI, "Sulmona.")

MANITIUS, M. "Beiträge zur Geschichte des Ovidius und anderer Römischer Schriftsteller im Mittelalter" in *Philologus, Supplementband*, VII. 723–767 (1899).

NINO, A. DE, *Ovidio nella tradizione popolare di Sulmona*. Casalbordino, 1886.

NITZE, W. A., AND DARGAN, E. P., *A History of French Literature*. New York, 1922. (See Part I, "The Middle Ages").

PARIS, G. DE, *La Littérature Française au Moyen Age*⁵. Paris, 1914.

SANDYS, J. E., *A History of Classical Scholarship*. 3 vols. Cambridge, England, 1903–1908. Vol. I³ (1921), pp. 638 ff.

SCHEVILL, R.: See under V.

SCHROETTER, W., *Ovid und die Troubadours*. Halle, 1908.

SYMONDS, J. A., *Wine, Women and Song*. London, 1884.

BIBLIOGRAPHY

V. Ovid in the Renaissance and Modern Times.

CANDY, H. C. H., *Some Newly Discovered Stanzas written by John Milton on Engraved Scenes illustrating Ovid's Metamorphoses*. London, 1924.

CAWLEY, F. S., "An Ovidian Prototype of a Character in 'Wilhelm Meister,' " in *Modern Language Notes*, XL. 288–292 (1925).

COOPER, C. B., *Some Elizabethan Opinions of the Poetry and Character of Ovid*. (University of Chicago Dissertation), Menasha, Wisconsin, 1914.

COULTER, CORNELIA C., "The Genealogy of the Gods" [Boccaccio's], in *Vassar Mediaeval Studies*, 317–341 (1923).

HANFORD, J. H., "The Youth of Milton. An Interpretation of his Early Literary Development," in *Studies in Shakespeare, Milton and Donne* (by members of the English Department of the University of Michigan), 89–163 (1925).

HOOD, T. L., "Browning's Ancient Classical Sources," in *Harvard Studies in Classical Philology*, XXXIII. 153–156 (1922).

MUSTARD, W. P., *Classical Echoes in Tennyson*. New York, 1904, pp. 121–124.

NOLHAC, P., DE, *Pétrarque et l'Humanisme*. Paris, 1892, pp. 145 ff.

OSGOOD, C. G., *The Classical Mythology of Milton's English Poems*, in *Yale Studies in English*, VIII. New York, 1900.

RAND, E. K., "Milton in Rustication," in *The University of North Carolina Studies in Philology*, XIX. 109–135 (1922).

RIPERT, É.: See under I.

ROOT, R. K., *Classical Mythology in Shakespeare*, in *Yale Studies in English*, IX. New York, 1903.

SCHEVILL, R., *Ovid and the Renaissance in Spain*. Berkeley, California, 1913. (With an introduction on Ovid in the Middle Ages.)

SELLAR, W. Y.: See under I.

WRIGHT, F. A.: See under II.

22. LANGUAGE AND PHILOLOGY. *Roland G. Kent*, University of Pennsylvania.

23. AESCHYLUS AND SOPHOCLES. *J. T. Sheppard*, King's College, Cambridge.

24. GREEK RELIGION. *Walter Woodburn Hyde*, University of Pennsylvania.

25. ROMAN RELIGION. *Gordon J. Laing*, University of Chicago.

26. MYTHOLOGY. *Jane Ellen Harrison*, Newnham College, Cambridge.

27. THEORIES REGARDING THE IMMORTALITY OF THE SOUL. *Clifford H. Moore*, Harvard University.

28. STAGE ANTIQUITIES. *James Turney Allen*, University of California.

29. GREEK POLITICS. *Ernest Barker*, Cambridge.

30. ROMAN POLITICS. *Frank Frost Abbott*, Princeton University.

31. ROMAN LAW. *Roscoe Pound*, Harvard Law School.

32. ECONOMICS AND SOCIETY.

33. WARFARE BY LAND AND SEA. *Eugene S. McCartney*, University of Michigan.

34. THE GREEK FATHERS. *Roy J. Deferrari*, The Catholic University of America.

35. GREEK BIOLOGY AND MEDICINE. *Henry Osborn Taylor*, New York.

36. MATHEMATICS. *David Eugene Smith*, Teachers College, Columbia University.

37. AGRICULTURE AND THE LOVE OF NATURE. *H. R. Fairclough*, Leland Stanford Junior University.

38. ASTRONOMY AND ASTROLOGY. *Franz Cumont*, Brussels.

39. THE FINE ARTS. *Arthur Fairbanks*, formerly of the Museum of Fine Arts, Boston.

40. ARCHITECTURE. *Alfred M. Brooks*, Swarthmore College.

41. ENGINEERING. *Alexander P. Gest*, Philadelphia